LIFE WITH A HIGH-FUNCTIONING AUTISM CHILD

A Parent's Survival Guide

Almog Cohen

To my incredible children, Gal and Maayan—your strength, love, and unique perspectives inspire me every day. And to my beloved wife, Adi—your unwavering support and endless patience make everything possible. This book is for you, with all my love.

BEFORE THE GUIDE: THE STORY BEHIND OUR OWN SURVIVAL

My name is Almog Cohen, and like many parents, my story is one of love, challenges, and unexpected twists. I'm married to my incredible wife, Adi. Together, we've faced some of life's hardest battles. Adi has epilepsy and is also a cancer survivor, and through it all, she's been my rock, an inspiration of strength and resilience.

We have been blessed with two beautiful children—Maayan, our eldest, who is now 10, and Gal, who is 7. From the very beginning, we knew Maayan was different. There was something about him that set him apart, even as a baby. He was always incredibly curious, with a sharp mind and an intense focus on the things that fascinated him. But there was also something we couldn't quite put our finger on.

For the first few years, we didn't know what made him different. As parents, we tried to brush it off, telling ourselves every child grows at their own pace. But deep down, we always had this gnawing feeling that there was something more. It wasn't until Maayan was six that we seriously began to consider autism. We had him tested, and our suspicions were confirmed—he was on the autism spectrum, high-functioning.

Around the same time, we began to worry about Gal, our

younger son. He wasn't speaking by the age of three or four, which was worrying. I remember thinking that maybe Gal had developmental delays or what we feared might be some kind of intellectual disability. When we had him tested, the results were both surprising and overwhelming—Gal, too, had high-functioning autism. It took us time to realize that while he appeared to be lagging behind, he was, in fact, incredibly smart and talented in his own unique way.

Raising two children with autism has been one of the most difficult journeys of our lives. There were countless moments of confusion, frustration, and sheer exhaustion. At times, it felt like we were constantly battling the unknown, unable to find the right way to connect with our children. We often felt like failures as parents, wondering if we were doing something wrong.

But as the years went by, something shifted. We realized that the problem wasn't our children—it was us. We were so focused on trying to fit them into a mold of what we thought they should be, instead of accepting who they were and learning how to support them. Once we shifted our perspective and began to understand their world, everything changed.

Maayan, with his deep intellect and passion for knowledge, flourished once we gave him the freedom to explore his interests in his own way. Gal, who we once worried might be "slow," surprised us with his unique talents and brilliance once we stopped trying to compare him to others. Our children didn't need to change—we did.

This book is about that journey. It's about what we've learned as parents of two incredible children with high-functioning autism. It's about the struggles we've faced, the mistakes we've made, and the lessons that have shaped us along the way.

Once Maayan started attending a regular school in Israel, under the *shiluv* program (meaning "inclusion" in English), it quickly became clear that he was struggling. Social interactions were a constant challenge. He couldn't make friends, and when he did, he couldn't keep them. Worse, he became a target for bullying. We noticed that not only was he being bullied by other students, but we also felt that even the school staff treated him unfairly. They seemed to believe that there was nothing wrong with him, implying that the issues we were concerned about were simply "in our heads." This lack of support wasn't limited to the school. Even our families, perhaps in an attempt to comfort themselves or us, would say things like, "All kids go through this," as if to downplay Maayan's struggles. We felt isolated, not just by the school but by those closest to us, and it was heartbreaking.

One day, after living in the same house and community in central Israel—the very place I grew up—for nearly ten years, I asked Adi a question that would change everything. I had seen a video on YouTube about a school in the jungles of Koh Phangan, Thailand. The school was run by an incredible Iranian woman who had profound knowledge and love for children, especially those with autism. After months of watching Maayan come home from school in tears, once even saying he would prefer to die, I asked Adi, "What do you think about moving to Thailand for a better school and life experience for Maayan?" I was half expecting her to say I was crazy, that we couldn't uproot our lives for something so uncertain. But to my surprise, she said, "Let's do it!" Her immediate and supportive response shocked me. I had never imagined she'd be so open to such a drastic change.

Suddenly, we were selling all our belongings and preparing to move to a place I had only known from my wild teenage years. For me, Thailand had always been a party destination, not a place where I ever imagined raising children. Back then, the idea of moving with kids to a remote island seemed like something only the most daring would attempt. But despite the initial fears and the many unknowns, we took the plunge. It wasn't easy at first, but now, years later, I can confidently say it was one of the best decisions we ever made. The nature, freedom, and the unique educational experience in Thailand have made a world of difference for Maayan, and for our family as a whole. It allowed us the time and space to really connect with our kids, to learn about them, and to grow as a close-knit family.

I share this story not to suggest everyone needs to make a dramatic move like ours, but to introduce you to the journey that brought us here. The rest of this book will focus less on my personal story and more on practical advice and strategies to help you navigate the adventure of raising a high-functioning autism child. While this journey has changed my life in ways I never expected, I wouldn't trade it for anything. My kids have taught me more about patience, love, and what it truly means to be a parent than I ever thought possible. I can confidently say, being their father has made me a better person. And while autism can present challenges, it has also been a blessing, because it makes my children who they are. Changing that would change them, and I wouldn't want them to be anything other than exactly who they are.

Parenting a child with autism is a road full of twists and turns, but it's a road worth traveling. And I hope that by sharing our story, you will find comfort, inspiration, and maybe even a few helpful tools to navigate your own journey.

I hope you come to see your child as the wonderful gift they truly are, even though it can sometimes be difficult to do so. Accepting them as they are isn't always easy, but once you do, you'll realize that autism is just one part of what makes them so special and unique. It's part of their identity, and in embracing it, you can begin to appreciate the incredible qualities that make your child one of a kind.

I dedicate this book to my two wonderful children, Maayan and

Gal, who have taught me how to be a better father and continue to teach me something new every single day. For their patience, their love, and for all they have given me, I thank them deeply and wholeheartedly.

CHAPTER 1: INTRODUCTION: UNDERSTANDING HIGH-FUNCTIONING AUTISM

When you hear the term "autism," it's easy to fall into a web of misconceptions and stereotypes that don't fully reflect the reality for many children and their families. For those new to the world of autism, the landscape can seem overwhelming. There's often confusion about what the diagnosis means, how it will affect your child, and what the future holds. But as parents, one of the most important things we can do is understand that autism is not a one-size-fits-all label.

This book is not just about autism in a clinical sense. It's about high-functioning autism specifically, a form of autism spectrum disorder (ASD) where children have average or above-average intellectual abilities but struggle with communication, social interactions, and adapting to everyday life situations. Understanding the nuances of high-functioning autism is crucial, not just for our children but for ourselves as parents, as we learn to support them.

What is High-Functioning Autism?

High-functioning autism refers to individuals on the autism spectrum who can function independently in many areas of life, often with strong intellectual abilities or verbal skills. However, they still face challenges related to social communication, emotional regulation, and sometimes sensory processing.

The term "high-functioning" can be misleading. While it might suggest that the challenges these children face are somehow less significant, the truth is that high-functioning autism presents its own unique set of difficulties. These children are often expected to blend into typical environments—whether at school, in social settings, or even at home—because they appear "normal" on the surface. But just because their struggles aren't immediately visible doesn't mean they aren't very real.

High-functioning autism can affect how a child interacts with others, responds to changes in routine, and processes sensory information. Many children with high-functioning autism are highly intelligent and may even have specific talents or areas of expertise, but they might struggle with everyday social cues, maintaining friendships, or managing overwhelming environments.

Common Misconceptions

One of the biggest challenges for families raising a child with high-functioning autism is navigating the misconceptions that others—sometimes even well-meaning family members, friends, or teachers—may have. These misunderstandings can make it harder for parents to find the support they need. Let's clear up some of the most common misconceptions:

"They don't look autistic." High-functioning autism is often invisible to the untrained eye. Your child may not exhibit the more obvious traits associated with severe autism, such as nonverbal behavior or repetitive movements, which can lead people to downplay their struggles. But just because a child doesn't "look autistic" doesn't mean they don't face real challenges in their daily lives.

"They'll grow out of it." Many people assume that children with high-functioning autism will eventually grow out of their behaviors, especially if they are intelligent or verbal. While children can and do develop important coping mechanisms and life skills with the right support, autism is a lifelong condition. It's something your child will learn to manage, but it will always be a part of who they are.

"It's just a discipline problem." Because children with high-functioning autism may display behaviors like impulsivity, emotional outbursts, or difficulty following rules, these behaviors are often mistaken for a lack of discipline. This couldn't be further from the truth. These behaviors are often linked to underlying difficulties with emotional regulation, sensory processing, or anxiety.

Unique Challenges of High-Functioning Autism

Children with high-functioning autism are unique in that they often fall into a "gray zone." They may not require as many obvious accommodations as those with more severe forms of autism, yet they struggle in ways that are often misunderstood or overlooked. Some of the key challenges include:

Social Interactions: One of the hallmark features of autism is difficulty with social communication. Children with high-functioning autism may struggle to understand social cues, make and keep friends, or engage in conversations. They might take things literally or have difficulty understanding sarcasm, jokes, or the unwritten rules of social interaction.

Emotional Regulation: Children with high-functioning autism often have intense emotions that can feel overwhelming. They might struggle with managing frustration, anxiety, or disappointment, leading to emotional outbursts or meltdowns that seem disproportionate to the situation. They may also have difficulty understanding or expressing their own emotions, making it hard for them to communicate when they are feeling upset or stressed.

Sensory Sensitivities: Many children with high-functioning autism experience sensory sensitivities, whether it's being overwhelmed by loud noises, bright lights, certain textures, or crowded spaces. These sensitivities can make everyday environments, such as school, extremely challenging.

Executive Functioning: Executive functioning refers to the set of skills that help us plan, organize, and complete tasks. Children with high-functioning autism often struggle with these skills, making it difficult for them to follow multi-step instructions, manage time effectively, or handle transitions between activities.

Strengths of Children with High-Functioning Autism

While high-functioning autism brings challenges, it's equally important to recognize the incredible strengths and talents that many children on the spectrum possess. These strengths are often overlooked because of a focus on the difficulties, but they can be the key to helping your child thrive.

Deep Focus and Passion: Many children with high-functioning autism have the ability to focus intensely on subjects or activities they're passionate about. Whether it's math, science, art, or a specific hobby, this intense focus can lead to incredible achievements and deep knowledge in a particular area.

Attention to Detail: Children on the autism spectrum often have a remarkable ability to notice details that others might miss. This can make them particularly skilled at tasks that require precision and careful observation.

Honesty and Integrity: Children with high-functioning autism tend to be very honest and straightforward. They may not always understand social conventions like white lies, but their honesty can be refreshing and can lead to deep, genuine connections with those who understand them.

Unique Perspectives: Autism allows children to see the world in ways that are different from neurotypical children. This unique perspective can foster creativity, innovation, and problem-solving abilities that stand out in remarkable ways.

Setting the Tone for the Journey Ahead

This book is not about a diagnosis—it's about understanding your child in a way that helps you support their growth, strengths, and challenges. High-functioning autism comes with its hurdles, but it also offers an opportunity to see the world through your child's eyes—a world that, while different, is filled with potential, creativity, and brilliance.

Throughout the following chapters, we'll explore the practical side of raising a child with high-functioning autism: how to recognize the signs, navigate school life, manage social interactions, and build a home environment that supports your child's needs. You'll find tips and strategies that we've learned along the way, both from our own experiences and from the wisdom of others who have walked this path before us.

Above all, this book is meant to be a supportive guide, offering not only practical advice but also a sense of hope. Raising a child with high-functioning autism isn't easy, but it can be an incredibly rewarding journey—one that challenges you, teaches you, and ultimately deepens the bond between you and your child.

CHAPTER 2: RECOGNIZING THE SIGNS: OUR FIRST CLUES

As parents, we walk into this journey armed with hopes, dreams, and expectations for our children. We imagine how they'll grow, reach milestones, and begin to interact with the world around them. But for some of us, those milestones don't come in the way we expect, and the path forward becomes filled with questions. For parents of children with high-functioning autism or ADHD or both, the signs often reveal themselves slowly, sometimes subtly, and sometimes through moments of profound difficulty. Recognizing these early signs is the first critical step toward understanding your child's unique needs and offering the right support.

Early Behavioral Signs: When Things Don't Fit the Mold

For many children with high-functioning autism or ADHD, the signs appear early but are easy to miss or dismiss. Every child develops at their own pace, and there's a wide range of "normal" when it comes to early childhood behaviors. However, there are certain patterns that may indicate something more.

In our case, Maayan, from the day he was born, was different from what we had expected. He was incredibly alert as a baby, rarely slept through the night, and always seemed like he was observing the world intensely. At first, we didn't think much of it. "Some babies are just alert," we told ourselves. But as the sleepless nights turned into sleepless months, and Maayan began showing signs of intense restlessness during the day, we started to realize something wasn't quite right.

One common sign of high-functioning autism or ADHD is

difficulty with sleep. Like Maayan, many children with these conditions struggle to fall asleep or stay asleep. Their minds are often racing, even at a young age, and it's difficult for them to wind down. This can lead to chronic exhaustion—for both the child and the parents.

For other children, early signs may include a high level of irritability or difficulty with transitions. If a toddler struggles with small changes in routine or has frequent tantrums that seem disproportionate to the situation, this could be an early indication of sensory overload or difficulty regulating emotions—both common in children with autism and ADHD.

Tip: Keep a journal of your child's behaviors, particularly those that seem unusual or persistent. Tracking patterns over time can help you spot potential signs and give you something concrete to discuss with professionals later on.

Another great tip for addressing the sleep issues I mentioned earlier, and one that I believe has changed our lives, is melatonin. It's known to be lacking in the brains of autistic children. I will discuss this in more detail in the upcoming chapters.

Social Clues: The Quiet Struggles

One of the most challenging aspects for many parents is recognizing the subtle signs of social difficulties in their children. While some children with autism or ADHD may display obvious behavioral differences, others, particularly those with high-functioning autism, may blend in well enough that their struggles aren't immediately apparent to outsiders. For us, this was the case with Maayan. He was academically advanced, incredibly curious, and had a remarkable memory, which made it easy to overlook his struggles in other areas.

But socially, he was lost. He didn't seem to understand how to interact with other children, and though he longed for friendships, he couldn't keep them. At birthday parties or playdates, he would either isolate himself or act out in frustration when things didn't go as he expected. As parents, we often interpreted this as misbehavior or stubbornness. It wasn't until later that we understood it was his way of dealing with the overwhelming complexity of social interactions.

Other children may exhibit different social signs. They might avoid eye contact, not respond to their name being called, or seem indifferent to social engagement. Alternatively, they might want to interact but lack the tools to do so effectively. Some children with high-functioning autism can be highly verbal but struggle with the nuances of conversation, often dominating discussions without picking up on social cues.

Tip: Watch for patterns in social behavior. Does your child seem uninterested in playing with others, or do they seem overwhelmed by social situations? Do they have difficulty maintaining eye contact or reading facial expressions? These could be signs of a broader issue.

Sensory Sensitivities: The World Feels Too Loud

One of the more distinct signs of autism or ADHD can be a heightened sensitivity to sensory input. Children with sensory processing difficulties may be overly sensitive to noise, light, textures, or even smells. In Gal's case, loud noises, like a vacuum cleaner or a crowded room, would send him into a state of distress. He would cover his ears, scream, or lash out in frustration, leaving us bewildered and exhausted. At the time, we didn't realize these were signs of sensory overload—a common experience for children on the autism spectrum.

Other children may react differently. Some may seek out sensory stimulation, constantly moving, fidgeting, or even crashing into things in an attempt to satisfy their sensory needs. This is common in children with ADHD, who often display hyperactivity or impulsivity as they navigate their environment.

Tip: Observe how your child reacts to sensory input. Are they particularly sensitive to certain noises, lights, or textures? Do they seem to seek out or avoid certain sensations? Understanding these sensory triggers can help you create a more comfortable environment for them.

Speech and Communication Delays

Speech delays are often one of the first noticeable signs that something is different. Gal, our younger son, didn't speak much by the time he was three or four. He would occasionally babble or say a few words, but his language development was far behind where it should have been. At first, we worried that he might have a developmental delay, or even worse, an intellectual disability. But what we didn't realize at the time was that delayed speech, particularly in combination with other behaviors, can be a sign of high-functioning autism.

For some children, language develops later than usual, but when it does, it often emerges in a more structured, formal way. Children with high-functioning autism might speak in complex sentences, but struggle with the back-and-forth of conversation. Others may have difficulty with non-verbal communication, like understanding gestures, facial expressions, or tone of voice.

Tip: If your child is not meeting typical language milestones, or if they display unusual communication patterns (like repeating phrases, or speaking in a monotone voice), it's worth discussing these concerns with a speech therapist or pediatrician.

The Importance of Trusting Your Instincts

One of the hardest parts of recognizing the signs of autism or ADHD in your child is trusting your instincts when others might downplay your concerns. In our case, we heard the same well-meaning but dismissive comments from family and friends: "Oh, he's just shy," or "All kids go through phases like this." It's easy to cling to the hope that everything will work itself out. After all, no parent wants to believe that their child might be struggling in ways they don't fully understand.

But as the months and years go by, those little doubts can turn into a persistent gnawing feeling that something isn't right. It's important to listen to that feeling, no matter how uncomfortable it might be. Early intervention can make a huge difference in a child's development, whether they have autism, ADHD, or any other neurodivergence.

Tip: If you suspect that your child may be showing signs of autism or ADHD, don't hesitate to seek a professional evaluation. While it can be difficult to face the unknown, getting answers early on can open the door to support systems, therapies, and strategies that will help your child thrive.

Seeing the Bigger Picture

Recognizing the signs of high-functioning autism or ADHD is often a long and emotional process. There are no clear-cut answers, and every child is different. But as you begin to connect the dots—from sleep issues, to social challenges, to sensory sensitivities—you start to see a bigger picture. Understanding that your child experiences the world in their own unique way is the first step toward helping them thrive.

CHAPTER 3: BUILDING A SUPPORT SYSTEM

Raising a child with high-functioning autism is both rewarding and challenging. As parents, we quickly realize that we can't do it all on our own. Building a strong support system is essential—not just for our children, but for us as parents, too. This chapter will explore the importance of creating a reliable, compassionate team around your child and family, and how critical it is for parents to stay actively involved in their child's life.

The Nuclear Family: Your Child's Most Important Support System

In our journey, one of the most significant changes we made as a family was realizing the importance of being present. For years, I worked in the high-tech industry, clocking long hours—9AM to 9PM, almost daily. My focus was on my career, and while I believed I was providing for my family financially, I slowly came to realize that my time and presence were equally important for my children, especially my oldest son.

Once we realized that Maayan, our eldest, would need more support than we initially anticipated, I made a huge decision. I closed my office and started working from home. This shift happened around the time Maayan started kindergarten . Soon after, we made the life-altering decision to move our family to an island in Thailand, seeking a more relaxed, family-centered lifestyle. We didn't just move physically; we began a journey together as a family—spending time together, not just in our free moments, but even during everyday routines.

Over time, we came to understand that the most critical support system for our children wasn't doctors or teachers—it was us, their nuclear family. Being close allowed us to truly see their needs, be better parents, and establish a deeper connection. While I don't suggest that every parent quit their job and move to a faraway island, I do recommend making an intentional effort to be a big part of your child's life. Understanding your child's needs requires being present during their critical moments—both the highs and the lows. Being a role model and creating a close, supportive system can make a world of difference.

One practice that we've maintained for years and has been transformative is our weekly "fun days." Every week, my wife and I each spend one-on-one time with one of our children. This special day, which our kids call "yes" days, is a time when they get to choose what we do, and we mostly say yes to their ideas. These days have become a cornerstone in our relationship with our kids, building trust and creating emotional space for them to open up. After a while, we started hearing things they wouldn't normally tell us—like how they felt about certain situations or experiences, about bullying at school. This simple tradition has had a profound impact on their emotional well-being and our connection with them.

Building a Team: Doctors, Therapists, and Teachers

While the family forms the heart of your child's support system, it's equally important to build a professional team to address the specific needs of your child's development. Navigating the complexities of high-functioning autism requires a multi-disciplinary approach, with each professional contributing their expertise to support your child in different areas of life.

The Importance of Choosing Your Case Manager

One of the most critical decisions you'll make in building a support team for your child is choosing the right case manager. This individual will serve as the main coordinator of your child's care and treatment plan, helping to organize the various professionals involved, from doctors to therapists to teachers. In most cases, this role is best suited for an emotional psychologist—someone who has a deep understanding of both your child's developmental needs and the emotional landscape of your family.

A good case manager does more than just manage appointments and reports. They act as the central figure in your child's care, ensuring that everyone involved in the treatment plan is aligned and working toward the same goals. This person should be someone you feel comfortable with and trust, as they will meet with both the child and parents separately, gaining a holistic understanding of the challenges and emotions involved.

The emotional psychologist in this role will often be the first line of support for both you and your child. They can help you navigate difficult moments, provide insights into your child's behavior, and offer guidance on how to communicate effectively with other professionals. They also act as an advocate for your child, ensuring that all therapists, doctors, and teachers are aware of your child's progress, needs, and any adjustments that should be made in their care plan. Choosing the right case manager can make a world of difference in how smoothly the treatment process runs and how supported you feel throughout the journey.

Doctors and Specialists: Your child's pediatrician or a developmental specialist will likely be your first point of contact after a diagnosis. They can refer you to the right professionals for further evaluations and therapies. A developmental psychologist or psychiatrist may help with emotional and behavioral challenges, while a neurologist may address any related conditions, like ADHD or sensory processing issues.

Therapists: Occupational therapists, speech therapists, and behavioral therapists all play an essential role in supporting children with autism. An occupational therapist can help your child develop fine motor skills, manage sensory sensitivities, and work on life skills. Speech therapists can assist with communication challenges, while behavioral therapists can guide your child in developing coping strategies for emotional regulation and social interactions.

Teachers and School Support: Your child's teachers and school staff are a vital part of the support system, especially when it comes to daily academic and social life. It's important to build a strong, communicative relationship with your child's teachers to ensure that they understand your child's unique needs. If your child has an Individualized Education Plan (IEP) or is part of an inclusion program, regular communication with the school will ensure that your child receives the appropriate accommodations and support.

Finding Support Groups: Online and Local Communities

The journey of raising a child with high-functioning autism can often feel isolating, especially when you feel like you're the only one dealing with certain challenges. That's where support groups can be life-changing. Connecting with other parents who are on similar journeys can provide a much-needed sense of community, understanding, and shared experience.

Online Support Groups: There are countless online forums, Facebook groups, and websites dedicated to supporting parents of children with autism. These communities allow you to share your experiences, ask for advice, and find emotional support from people who truly understand what you're going through. Whether you're looking for tips on navigating school systems or simply need a place to vent, these groups offer a valuable resource.

Local Support Groups: Many cities and towns have local support groups where parents can meet in person to share experiences and provide support to one another. These groups can be especially helpful for building connections in your community and learning about local resources such as therapists, special education programs, or recreational activities for children with autism.

Tip: Don't hesitate to reach out to a local autism support organization or your child's doctor for recommendations on reliable online and local support groups. These connections can provide invaluable insights and help you feel less alone.

Communicating Effectively with Family and Friends

One of the more challenging aspects of building a support system is communicating your child's needs to family and friends who may not fully understand autism. It's common for extended family members or friends to misinterpret behaviors or offer well-meaning but unhelpful advice, especially when they don't understand what your child is going through.

To foster understanding and support within your circle, it's important to communicate openly about your child's challenges, as well as their strengths. Be clear about your expectations and how family members can contribute to your child's well-being. This may include educating them about your child's sensory sensitivities, social struggles, or the importance of routine.

Here are some strategies for effective communication:

Be Open About Your Child's Needs: Explain what high-functioning autism is and how it affects your child. Share specific examples of behaviors they might see and how they can help. This can reduce misunderstandings and ensure that your child is supported in family settings.

Ask for Patience and Understanding: Let your family and friends know that certain behaviors, like meltdowns or social withdrawal, aren't intentional or "bad" behavior. Ask them to be patient and understanding, and to approach your child with empathy.

Set Boundaries When Necessary: Sometimes, family or friends may struggle to understand your child's needs, despite your efforts. In these cases, it's okay to set boundaries to protect your child's well-being. It's also okay to seek support elsewhere, if certain relationships feel draining or unhelpful.

CHAPTER 4: STRONG PARENTS, STRONG CHILDREN: THE FOUNDATION OF A HEALTHY MARRIAGE

It might seem unusual to focus on marriage and personal relationships in a book about raising children with high-functioning autism, but the truth is, this chapter belongs here at the start for a reason—it's one of the most important factors in your child's well-being. Raising a child with autism, with all the therapies, appointments, and challenges that come along with it, requires an immense amount of time and emotional energy. And while it's natural for parents to pour themselves into their children's needs, there's a hidden cost: the risk of losing ourselves and our relationships in the process.

As parents, we often forget that in order to be the best caregivers for our children, we need to be in a good place ourselves. This chapter focuses on one of the most essential—and often overlooked—parts of raising a child with high-functioning autism: maintaining a strong, healthy relationship with your partner and yourself. Your marriage, or partnership, is the foundation upon which your child's sense of security, stability, and well-being is built. If that foundation cracks under the pressure of day-to-day stress and exhaustion, it can ripple through your family, affecting your children in ways you might not expect.

The Risk of Losing Ourselves in the Process

In our journey, my wife and I quickly realized how easy it was for all our free time to be consumed by Maayan's needs. There were therapy appointments, school meetings, playdates, and social skill groups. As parents of two children with autism, it felt like we were always in motion, managing schedules and making sure our boys had the support they needed. Our own needs, however, seemed to fade into the background. The quiet dinners we used to enjoy, the weekends spent together, and the small moments of connection that we once cherished all disappeared, replaced by the overwhelming demands of parenting.

I was working long hours, often from 9 AM to 9 PM in the office, trying to balance my career with my family life. At some point, it became clear that this wasn't sustainable. After my oldest son went to first grade, we made the life-altering decision to move our family to an island in Thailand. This decision wasn't just about seeking a slower pace of life for our children; it was about our family's survival—both as individuals and as a unit.

By being physically and emotionally present for each other and our children, we started to understand the depth of our children's needs. But more importantly, we came to realize that if we weren't taking care of ourselves and our relationship, we wouldn't have the emotional energy or stability to be the kind of parents our children needed. The same is true for any parent—whether you're in Thailand or anywhere else in the world. You don't have to make dramatic changes, but you do need to recognize that you, as parents, are the foundation of your child's support system.

Prioritizing Your Relationship: Why It Matters

It's easy to fall into the trap of thinking that every spare moment should be spent focusing on your children, especially when they have special needs. But the reality is that if you and your partner neglect your relationship, it will impact your ability to parent effectively. Children are incredibly perceptive, and they pick up on the emotional tone of their home. If you and your partner are constantly stressed, disconnected, or unhappy, that tension will affect your children, even if it's never explicitly spoken about.

In fact, studies have shown that children—especially those

on the autism spectrum—thrive in environments where their parents maintain a strong, healthy relationship. The stability that comes from having parents who prioritize each other's well-being creates a sense of security for children. They learn from the relationship they observe, and in turn, develop healthier emotional responses and coping mechanisms.

One of the best ways to keep your relationship strong is to create regular opportunities for connection, away from the chaos of daily life. Schedule weekly "alone time" with your partner—time when you're not discussing therapies, school issues, or your child's progress, but focusing on each other. Go out to dinner, take a walk, watch a movie, or simply spend time together uninterrupted. It doesn't have to be extravagant, but it does need to be consistent.

Don't Forget Your Hobbies and Personal Freedom

One of the common struggles that many parents face, especially when raising children with autism, is the feeling that their personal lives and interests have to be sacrificed. Between work, family responsibilities, and therapies, it can seem like there's no time left for hobbies, exercise, or social activities. But as important as your children's needs are, your personal happiness and fulfillment are equally critical to your overall well-being—and, by extension, your ability to be a good parent.

You and your partner both need to find ways to continue enjoying the activities that bring you joy and a sense of freedom. Whether it's exercising, reading, painting, or spending time with friends, these personal outlets are vital for maintaining your emotional balance. They help reduce stress, prevent burnout, and give you the energy needed to support your child through their challenges.

If you let go of everything that brings you happiness and focus solely on your child's needs, you risk becoming emotionally drained. This can lead to resentment, frustration, and even conflict with your spouse. Instead, make a conscious effort to carve out time for yourselves—both individually and as a couple.

You don't need hours of free time every day, but even small moments, like a walk in the evening or a coffee break during the day, can help you recharge.

Spicing Up the Relationship: Keeping the Love Alive

When we become parents, especially in the context of raising children with special needs, it's easy to let romance take a back seat. But keeping the love alive between you and your partner is essential for maintaining a strong relationship. It's not just about scheduling date nights—it's about actively working to keep your connection vibrant and exciting.

This can mean planning a spontaneous weekend getaway, surprising your partner with something thoughtful, or simply making the effort to reconnect at the end of a long day. These small gestures go a long way in keeping your relationship healthy and ensuring that both partners feel valued and loved.

For us, keeping our relationship alive meant finding ways to stay connected, even when life felt overwhelming. Whether it was a simple conversation over coffee or planning a surprise "date night" after the kids went to bed, we made a conscious effort to prioritize each other. This not only strengthened our bond, but it also helped us approach parenting with a renewed sense of partnership.

Happy Parents, Happy Children

At the end of the day, the most important takeaway is this: happy, content parents are essential for raising happy, content children. When we prioritize our own relationship and well-being, we create a strong foundation that supports our entire family. Parenting a child with autism is demanding, but it doesn't have to come at the cost of your personal happiness or your relationship with your spouse.

By investing time and energy into your marriage and personal life, you'll not only improve your own well-being, but you'll also provide your children with a stable, loving environment where they can thrive. So, while the demands of raising a child with autism may sometimes feel all-consuming, don't forget to nurture your own happiness—and your relationship. Your children need you to be happy, healthy, and whole, so you can give them the love and support they deserve.

For Single Parents: Prioritizing Yourself and Your Happiness

It's important to acknowledge that not every family has two parents navigating this journey together. If you're a single parent raising a child with high-functioning autism, the challenges may feel even more overwhelming at times. Without a partner to share the load, it's easy to feel like you have to sacrifice everything—your free time, your hobbies, and especially your personal life. But just like parents in a relationship, single parents need to prioritize their own happiness and well-being.

If you're a single parent, don't feel guilty about making time for yourself. This includes pursuing hobbies, socializing with friends, and yes, even dating. Finding the right balance can be tricky, but it's important to create space for your own needs. Building a strong support network of friends, family, or even a babysitter who understands your child's needs can give you the time to recharge and explore relationships. Dating as a single parent isn't just about finding a new partner—it's about making sure you continue to live a fulfilling life, one where you feel supported and loved. When you're happy and grounded in your personal life, it reflects positively on your children, showing them that their parent is resilient, capable, and deserving of joy, just like they are.

CHAPTER 5: DAILY ROUTINES: ESTABLISHING STRUCTURE AND CONSISTENCY

Children with high-functioning autism thrive in environments that are structured and predictable. For them, routines are not just about creating order in their day—they provide a sense of safety, stability, and comfort in a world that can often feel overwhelming and unpredictable. Establishing consistent daily routines is one of the most powerful tools you can use to help your child manage their emotions, behaviors, and transitions throughout the day.

For parents of children with high-functioning autism, creating and sticking to routines might seem like an extra task in an already busy day. However, routines help reduce stress—for both you and your child—and provide a framework within which your child can feel more in control of their surroundings. Children on the autism spectrum often struggle with transitions, but predictable routines can make these transitions easier and less anxiety-inducing.

The Importance of Routines for Children with High-Functioning Autism

For many children with high-functioning autism, the world can feel chaotic and overwhelming. They may struggle with sensory sensitivities, social interactions, and changes in their environment, all of which can contribute to feelings of anxiety. Routines provide a way to mitigate that anxiety by creating a predictable, consistent flow to the day. When a child knows what to expect and when, it helps them feel more in control of their environment, which in turn reduces stress.

Routines also play a crucial role in helping children develop important life skills. By establishing consistent habits for tasks like getting dressed, brushing teeth, or completing homework, parents are teaching their children how to manage time, stay organized, and take responsibility. Over time, this consistency fosters greater independence, as children begin to understand what is expected of them and how to complete tasks on their own.

Now, don't get me wrong—this won't be easy, especially with a high-functioning autistic child. "High-functioning" doesn't mean they're easier to manage. Like any other child, they may resist things like taking a shower or brushing their teeth. And for many autistic children, sensory issues can make everyday tasks even more challenging, like the feeling of water pouring over their head. But despite these difficulties, it's crucial to stick to routines. While neurotypical children might be able to skip tasks here and there without disrupting the household, for autistic children, maintaining structure and organization is essential. The stability of a routine provides comfort, even if it's difficult at times to enforce.

For parents, routines create a structure that helps the entire family stay organized. It can be difficult to juggle the demands of daily life—school, work, therapy sessions, social activities—without a plan in place. By implementing consistent routines, parents can ensure that their child's needs are met while also making time for their own well-being.

Practical Strategies for Establishing Morning, School, and Bedtime Routines

Creating daily routines doesn't have to be complicated. The key is to make routines predictable, consistent, and tailored to your child's specific needs and preferences. Here are some strategies for establishing routines for different parts of the day:

Morning Routine

The morning can set the tone for the entire day. For many children with autism, the transition from sleeping to waking up and getting ready for school can be particularly difficult. Having a predictable morning routine helps ease this transition and gets the day started on the right foot.

Visual Schedules: Children with autism often respond well to visual aids. Create a morning routine chart with pictures or icons that represent each step of the process—getting dressed, brushing teeth, eating breakfast, putting on shoes, and heading to school. This provides a clear, visual reminder of what comes next and reduces anxiety around transitions.

Online Task Tables: In our home, we created an online task table that each child can view on their iPad. The table consists of daily tasks like brushing teeth, going to school on time, eating breakfast, and more. The table serves as both a schedule and a way to track their progress, reinforcing the structure of the morning. Each child knows exactly what is expected of them, and they can check off tasks as they complete them.

Positive Reinforcement: It's important to give positive feedback for tasks completed, even if they're small. If your child successfully brushes their teeth or gets dressed on their own, acknowledge it: "Great job getting ready this morning!" Praise helps build confidence and encourages them to stick to the routine.

School Routine

For children with high-functioning autism, school can be a challenging environment. Having a routine in place for both getting to school and managing school-related tasks at home can help your child feel more secure and confident in navigating the school day.

Preparing for School the Night Before: To reduce morning stress, prepare everything the night before—clothes, school supplies, and lunch. This not only saves time but also minimizes unexpected changes in the morning routine that could cause anxiety.

Post-School Decompression: Many children with autism need time to decompress after a long day at school. Build a routine for when they get home, such as giving them 30 minutes of quiet time before diving into homework or chores. This gives them the space to unwind and process the day in a calm, predictable way.

Bedtime Routine

Establishing a consistent bedtime routine is crucial for children with high-functioning autism, especially if they struggle with sleep. A well-structured bedtime routine helps signal that the day is coming to an end and prepares the body and mind for sleep.

Wind-Down Activities: About 30 minutes before bedtime, begin quiet, calming activities like reading a book, doing a puzzle, or listening to soft music. These activities should be part of a consistent routine that helps your child relax.

Use Visual Aids: Just like the morning routine, create a visual bedtime schedule. Include tasks like taking a bath, putting on pajamas, brushing teeth, and getting into bed. Following the same steps in the same order each night makes the bedtime process smoother and more predictable.

Reward Systems: For bedtime, rewards can be a great way to encourage your child to follow the routine. In our household, we created a reward system using an online table. Our children know that they need to complete certain tasks—like brushing their teeth, getting ready for bed, and sleeping through the night—to earn points. These points accumulate and lead to small surprises or rewards.

The Importance of Structure, Tables, and Rewards

One of the most effective strategies we've found for maintaining routines and motivating our children is through the use of structured tables and reward systems. Autistic children often thrive on structure and clear expectations, and incorporating tables, checklists, or visual schedules into their daily routine can provide that sense of order.

In our case, we created an online task table that both of our children can access on their iPads. This table is divided into days of the week and includes standard tasks like brushing teeth, going to school on time, eating meals together, and taking a shower. The table has eight activities listed for each day, but the goal is for each child to complete at least six tasks to earn a small reward in the evening, like a small toy or a treat.

However, we understand that children aren't soldiers—they won't always complete every task exactly as expected. That's why we included a system where they can "save" their reward for the day by completing an extra activity. For example, if they miss a task, they can help around the house or complete a page from a workbook to make up for it. This ensures that they still feel successful, even if they didn't get everything done.

The goal isn't to be rigid or harsh with these routines but to give children a sense of accomplishment and control over their day. By offering flexibility and additional opportunities to succeed, we avoid making our kids feel like failures. Instead, they learn that there's always a way to recover from small setbacks, which is a powerful lesson in resilience.

Don't forget to give praise and positive feedback for the small things. Saying something as simple as "Wow, you did a great job putting away your toys!" can have a big impact on your child's self-esteem. Celebrating small successes lays the foundation for bigger achievements down the road.

Handling Transitions and Changes in Routine

While routines are essential, life is unpredictable, and changes in routine are inevitable. For children with high-functioning autism, these disruptions can be particularly stressful, but there are strategies to help ease the transitions:

Prepare in Advance: If you know a change in routine is coming—like a doctor's appointment or a family trip—prepare your child in advance. Explain the change in simple, clear terms, and if possible, use visual aids or social stories to help them understand what will happen.

Offer Choices: When routines need to change, offering your child choices can help them feel more in control. For example, if their usual bedtime routine will be disrupted, let them choose which part of the routine they'd like to keep, such as picking out their pajamas or choosing a bedtime story.

Stay Calm and Reassuring: When a routine is disrupted, your child may feel anxious or overwhelmed. In these moments, it's important to remain calm and offer reassurance. Let them know that it's okay for things to change sometimes and that you'll help them through it.

Do Not Promise What You Can't Keep: One key to managing expectations is to avoid telling your child about events or activities you aren't certain will happen. Try not to promise activities if you're unsure whether you'll have the time or energy to follow through. Waiting for confirmation before preparing your child can help avoid unnecessary disappointment. Of course, there will always be unforeseen changes that are out of our control, and flexibility is needed. However, as a rule, I try to only inform my children about things that are almost guaranteed to happen. This way, we can prevent some of the emotional distress that comes with unexpected cancellations or changes.

CHAPTER 6: MANAGING SENSORY OVERLOAD AND ANXIETY

Children with high-functioning autism often experience the world in ways that may seem overwhelming or even chaotic to neurotypical individuals. Sensory sensitivities and anxiety can play a significant role in their day-to-day lives, making it difficult to navigate even the simplest environments like home, school, or public spaces. Understanding these sensory challenges and developing strategies to manage anxiety is crucial for creating a more comfortable, supportive environment for your child.

Understanding Sensory Sensitivities and Their Impact on Behavior

Sensory sensitivities are common in children with autism, particularly those on the high-functioning end of the spectrum. These children can have heightened or diminished responses to sensory input, such as light, sound, texture, or temperature. What may seem like minor irritations to a neurotypical person—bright lights, loud noises, or certain fabrics—can feel overwhelming and even unbearable to a child with autism.

Sensory overload occurs when your child's senses are bombarded by too much input at once, leading to discomfort, frustration, or meltdowns. This isn't about bad behavior or a lack of discipline—sensory overload is a genuine physical and emotional response to an overwhelming environment. It's important to understand that when a child is experiencing sensory overload, they aren't being difficult or defiant—they are trying to cope with a situation that feels overwhelming to them.

Sensory issues can also be linked to anxiety. For many children, the fear of being in a situation where sensory overload might occur can lead to heightened anxiety, making it hard to relax or focus, even in seemingly calm environments. Being aware of your child's specific sensory sensitivities is the first step toward helping them manage these challenges.

Tips for Managing Sensory Overload at Home, School, and in Public

While you can't eliminate all sensory triggers from your child's environment, there are ways to manage them more effectively and help your child feel more in control. The following tips offer practical strategies for creating sensory-friendly environments at home, school, and in public spaces:

At Home

Home should be a safe, comfortable space where your child feels in control of their surroundings. You can create a sensory-friendly environment at home by considering your child's specific triggers and adjusting accordingly.

Create a Sensory Retreat: Designate a quiet, calming space in your home where your child can go when they feel overwhelmed. This space should be free from loud noises, harsh lighting, or other sensory triggers. Fill the space with comforting objects like soft blankets, noise-cancelling headphones, or weighted blankets that help your child feel grounded and safe.

Use Calming Sensory Tools: Having sensory tools on hand can make a big difference when your child is feeling overloaded. Items like stress balls, fidget toys, or soft fabric swatches can provide tactile stimulation that helps calm their senses. For some children, aromatherapy with calming scents like lavender or chamomile can also help create a soothing atmosphere.

Adjust Lighting and Sound: Many children with autism are sensitive to bright lights or loud noises. Use dimmable lights, blackout curtains, or lamps with soft lighting in areas where your child spends the most time. Consider using white noise machines or calming background music to mask disruptive sounds and create a peaceful environment.

At School

School environments can be particularly overwhelming due to their unpredictable nature and the variety of sensory inputs children are exposed to—loud bells, crowded hallways, and fluorescent lighting, to name a few. Advocating for your child's sensory needs in school can make a big difference in their ability to cope.

Communicate with Teachers: Work closely with your child's teachers to ensure they understand your child's sensory sensitivities. Ask if your child can have access to a quiet space where they can go if they feel overwhelmed. This could be a designated area in the classroom or a resource room where they can take sensory breaks during the day.

Sensory-Friendly Tools at School: Make sure your child has access to sensory tools that can help them self-regulate during the school day. For example, noise-cancelling headphones can help block out loud classroom noises, while fidget toys can keep their hands busy without distracting others. Some children benefit from using a small, portable sensory kit that includes calming items they can access as needed.

Structured Routines: Children with high-functioning autism often do best in structured environments with predictable routines. Work with your child's teacher to establish a clear schedule for each day, including time for breaks and sensory relief. Having a visual schedule in the classroom can help reduce anxiety about what's coming next, giving your child a sense of control over their day.

In Public Spaces

Navigating public spaces can be a significant source of sensory overload for children with autism. Crowded areas, bright lights, unexpected sounds, and unfamiliar environments can all contribute to anxiety and discomfort. With some planning and preparation, however, these outings can become more manageable.

Plan Ahead: Before going to a busy public space, such as a shopping mall or a restaurant, prepare your child by explaining where you're going and what to expect. If possible, visit the location during a quieter time to reduce sensory input. Bringing along familiar sensory tools, like noise-cancelling headphones or a favorite toy, can also provide comfort in unfamiliar settings.

Use Social Stories: Social stories are simple, visual narratives that describe a situation and outline what will happen, step by step. They help children anticipate what to expect and reduce anxiety around transitions. If your child has difficulty with new environments, create a social story that explains the outing and what they will encounter.

Take Breaks: If your child becomes overwhelmed in a public space, don't be afraid to take breaks. Find a quiet area, like a restroom or car, where your child can decompress and reset before re-entering the situation. Sometimes, a short break is all that's needed to help them regain composure.

Some Places You Should Go on Your Own: Sometimes, the best decision is to not take your child to a place that may be too overwhelming for them. While we want our children to be able to go anywhere, there are some environments or events that simply aren't suitable for them, and it's okay to decide to go without them. For example, I used to take my kids to posh restaurants with my wife, but it quickly became clear they couldn't handle the long wait times or the formal setting. Every time we tried, it ended in frustration—our kids felt disappointed with themselves, and we were left angry and embarrassed. We learned to adjust by taking them to restaurants that had a playground or were near the beach, so they didn't have to sit and wait at the table for long. Every child is different, but if you know a certain place will be too hard for your child, and they don't really need to be there, consider going on your own or with other adults instead. It's okay to prioritize their comfort and well-being.

Practical Tools for Managing Anxiety

Alongside sensory sensitivities, anxiety is another common challenge for children with high-functioning autism. Anxiety can be triggered by changes in routine, unfamiliar situations, or the fear of sensory overload. Helping your child manage anxiety involves teaching them calming techniques and creating environments where they feel safe and supported.

Here are some practical tools to help manage anxiety:

Deep Breathing Exercises: One of the simplest and most effective ways to reduce anxiety is through deep breathing exercises. Teach your child how to take slow, deep breaths by inhaling through the nose for four counts, holding for four counts, and exhaling through the mouth for four counts. For younger children, you can use the phrase "smell the flower, then blow out the candle" to make the exercise more engaging and easier for them to understand. Practicing this regularly can help them calm down during moments of stress.

Progressive Muscle Relaxation: This technique involves tensing and then relaxing different muscle groups, starting from the feet and working up to the head. It helps release physical tension and is a great tool for children who struggle with anxiety-related body stress. You can guide your child through the exercise, helping them focus on how their body feels as they tense and relax each muscle group.

Visual Calming Techniques: Some children with high-functioning autism respond well to visual calming techniques. This could be something as simple as watching a calming video, using a sensory bottle filled with glitter or water, or looking at a favorite picture. These visual stimuli can provide a soothing focus and help reduce anxiety.

Create a Sensory-Friendly Environment: At home, create a space where your child can go when they're feeling anxious or overwhelmed. This could be a quiet corner of their room or a designated "calm down" area. Fill the space with calming sensory tools like weighted blankets, fidget toys, or soft lighting. Allowing your child to retreat to this space when needed gives them control over their environment and a safe place to manage their emotions.

Weighted Items: Weighted blankets or vests can provide a sense of security and grounding, helping children with autism feel more centered. The gentle pressure from weighted items can calm the nervous system and help reduce feelings of anxiety.

CHAPTER 7: NAVIGATING FOOD CHOICES FOR HIGH-FUNCTIONING AUTISTIC CHILDREN

One of the common challenges faced by parents of high-functioning autistic children is managing food preferences and sensitivities. Many children on the autism spectrum have limited textures they find appealing or narrow ranges of foods they're willing to eat. Often, they will fixate on a few specific foods, requesting them for every meal. As a parent, balancing your child's preferences while ensuring they receive proper nutrition can feel overwhelming.

In this section, I will explore the sensory issues related to food and offer strategies for helping your child maintain a healthy, balanced diet while respecting their food choices. We'll also share our personal approach, which includes having meals together as a family and offering a variety of options to encourage your child to try new foods on their own terms.

The Sensory Challenges of Eating

For many children with high-functioning autism, sensory sensitivities extend beyond what they feel, hear, or see—taste and texture can also be overwhelming. A child may refuse to eat certain foods because they dislike the texture, smell, or appearance, even if they've never tasted it. Foods that are too mushy, crunchy, or have mixed textures (like casseroles or stews) can trigger negative reactions, leading children to reject those foods outright.

It's important to recognize that these food preferences and aversions are often not about being "picky" or difficult. Instead, they reflect the child's sensory experience, which can be much more intense than it is for neurotypical children. Your child may genuinely find certain textures uncomfortable or certain smells overwhelming, leading them to stick to familiar, "safe" foods.

The Same Meal, Every Day

Many parents of high-functioning autistic children report that their child wants the same meal every day, sometimes for weeks or months on end. This is partly because of their need for routine and predictability, which extends to food choices. Eating the same meal can be comforting for them, offering a sense of control and familiarity in an otherwise unpredictable world.

While it's okay to honor these preferences, it's also essential to ensure your child is getting the right nutrition. For example, if your child only wants to eat pasta for every meal, you can start to vary the type of pasta or the sauce, slowly introducing different ingredients to expand their diet. It's important to be patient and not to force changes, as this could lead to more resistance.

Balancing Preferences and Nutrition

Finding the balance between letting your child eat what they want and ensuring they maintain a healthy diet can be tricky. Here are some strategies to help navigate this:

Gradual Introductions: Start by introducing new foods gradually, one at a time. For example, if your child loves chicken nuggets, try introducing a similar food, like homemade breaded chicken, that's just slightly different in texture. Over time, you can continue to adjust the flavors and textures, slowly broadening their food choices.

Mixing Favorites with New Foods: Pair a favorite food with something new. If your child only eats white rice, try serving it with a small portion of a new food on the side, like a vegetable or a protein they've never tried before. By keeping their favorite food on the plate, you provide comfort while gently introducing new options.

Smoothies and Hidden Nutrients: Some children with high-functioning autism are more open to eating pureed or blended foods. This can be a great way to sneak in extra nutrients. Smoothies can be a lifesaver—blend fruits, vegetables, and protein-rich ingredients into a drink that your child already enjoys. You can experiment with adding spinach, carrots, or avocado into a fruit-based smoothie without drastically changing the taste.

Food Exploration Through Play: Sometimes allowing your child to explore food without the pressure to eat can make a big difference. Encourage them to touch, smell, or even play with different foods in a low-pressure environment. This can help familiarize them with new textures and smells, making them more likely to try these foods later on.

Our Approach: Family Meals and Expanding Food Choices

In our household, we've found that the best way to help our children try new foods is by creating a supportive, low-pressure environment during family meals. Every evening, we have dinner together, and we place several options on the table. This gives our children the freedom to choose what they want to eat, while also subtly encouraging them to explore new tastes and textures.

For example, we might have a plate of familiar foods, like pasta or chicken, but we also include small portions of new or less familiar foods. The key is not to force them to try anything, but to give them the option. Over time, we noticed that they began to experiment with new foods at their own pace, on their own terms. It might start with a nibble, and eventually, they'll add a new item to their preferred list of foods.

We've also found that giving our children control over their choices helps reduce anxiety around food. For instance, if they're not in the mood for a particular food one evening, they can choose something else from the options on the table. However, we also try to maintain a structure by encouraging them to try at least one new thing each week, even if it's just a small bite. This helps keep the door open for trying new foods without overwhelming them.

Creating a Healthy Food Environment

Here are some additional tips for ensuring your child gets the nutrition they need while accommodating their sensory sensitivities:

Offer Choices: Just as we do during our family meals, offering a variety of foods and letting your child choose can reduce anxiety and make them more likely to try something new. Instead of preparing one meal that might overwhelm them, give them two or three options they can choose from, allowing them to feel more in control.

Stick to a Routine: Children with high-functioning autism often thrive on routine, and this applies to mealtimes as well. Try to keep mealtimes consistent, with meals served at the same time each day. This predictability can help reduce anxiety around food and make your child feel more secure.

Avoid Food Battles: It's tempting to push your child to eat certain foods, especially when you're worried about their nutrition. However, forcing them to eat something they dislike or creating a stressful mealtime environment can backfire. It's more effective to gently encourage exploration while keeping mealtimes positive and relaxed.

Expanding the Food World, One Bite at a Time

Navigating food choices for high-functioning autistic children can be a long and sometimes frustrating process. However, with patience, understanding, and creativity, you can help broaden your child's palate while ensuring they receive the nutrients they need to grow and thrive. By creating a supportive and low-pressure environment, offering variety, and allowing your child to make their own choices, you can make mealtimes less stressful and more enjoyable for everyone.

Remember, every child is different. Some may take longer to try new foods, while others might be more open to experimentation. The goal is not to rush the process but to gently encourage them to explore the wide world of food, one bite at a time.

CHAPTER 8: NAVIGATING THE SCHOOL SYSTEM

Navigating the school system can be a complex and challenging experience for parents of high-functioning autistic children. School plays a significant role in your child's development, and ensuring they have the right support in place is crucial for their success both academically and socially. The traditional school environment, with its rigid structures and social dynamics, may not always suit the needs of children on the spectrum. That's why it's important to work closely with teachers, school administrators, and support staff to create a plan that allows your child to thrive.

Creating an Individualized Education Plan (IEP) or 504 Plan

An IEP or 504 Plan is a specific term used in the United States, but similar support systems exist in other countries, each with different names and approaches. For example, in the UK, these are known as Education, Health, and Care Plans (EHCPs), while in Canada, provinces have Individual Program Plans (IPPs), and in Australia, Individual Learning Plans (ILPs) are common. This section has been written with the US framework in mind, but it's important to note that each country has its own system and process for supporting children with special needs.

The first step in ensuring that your child receives the appropriate support in school is to create an IEP or 504 plan. Both of these plans are designed to provide accommodations and services to students with disabilities, helping them access the curriculum and participate fully in school life.

What Is an IEP?

An IEP is a legal document that outlines the specific special education services, supports, and accommodations your child will receive at school. It is created after a thorough evaluation of your child's strengths and challenges, and it includes goals tailored to their unique needs. The IEP process involves a team of professionals—including teachers, school psychologists, and sometimes therapists—who work with you to develop a plan that addresses your child's academic, social, and emotional needs.

What Is a 504 Plan?

A 504 plan is designed for students who do not require special education services but still need accommodations to access the curriculum. This could include things like extra time on tests, preferential seating, or access to a quiet room during stressful periods. While a 504 plan is not as comprehensive as an IEP, it is still an important tool for ensuring your child's needs are met in the classroom.

When deciding whether your child should have an IEP or 504 plan, it's important to consider the specific support they need. High-functioning autistic children may require services that range from speech therapy and occupational therapy to behavioral support and social skills training. Working closely with your child's school to determine the best approach will set the foundation for a successful school experience.

Key Steps to Creating an IEP or 504 Plan:

Request an Evaluation: If you believe your child needs an IEP or 504 plan, the first step is to request an evaluation from the school. This evaluation will assess your child's academic abilities, social skills, and any other areas of concern.

Participate in the Process: As a parent, you are a key member of the IEP or 504 team. Be actively involved in meetings, provide input on your child's strengths and challenges, and ensure that the plan is tailored to your child's individual needs.

Set Clear, Measurable Goals: Work with the school team to set specific, measurable goals for your child. These goals should address not only academic progress but also social and emotional development.

Review and Revise: An IEP or 504 plan is not static—it should be reviewed and updated regularly to reflect your child's progress and any changes in their needs. Don't hesitate to request adjustments if you feel the plan is not meeting your child's goals.

Working with Teachers and School Administrators

Once an IEP or 504 plan is in place, it's essential to maintain open communication with teachers and school administrators. Your child's success depends not only on the plan but also on the collaboration between you, the school staff, and any external professionals involved in your child's care.

Establishing a Relationship with Teachers: Take the time to meet with your child's teachers at the start of the school year. Share your child's IEP or 504 plan with them and discuss any specific accommodations your child will need. Be open about your child's strengths and areas where they may require extra support. The more information you can provide, the better equipped the teacher will be to meet your child's needs.

Be Proactive: Don't wait for problems to arise before you communicate with the school. Regularly check in with teachers and administrators to monitor your child's progress. If you notice any concerns, address them early. Staying proactive helps ensure that small issues don't become larger challenges.

Advocate for Your Child: As a parent, you are your child's strongest advocate. If you feel that your child's needs are not being met, don't hesitate to speak up. Whether it's requesting additional services or accommodations, or adjusting the goals in the IEP or 504 plan, it's important to ensure that your child's voice is heard and their needs are prioritized.

Helping Your Child Handle Schoolwork, Social Interactions, and Extracurricular Activities

In addition to academic accommodations, helping your child navigate social interactions and extracurricular activities is critical to their overall development. High-functioning autistic children often excel in certain academic areas but may struggle with social skills, handling transitions, or managing the pressure of extracurricular activities.

Managing Schoolwork

Schoolwork can be a source of anxiety for children on the spectrum, particularly if they are struggling to understand assignments, manage deadlines, or handle the sensory demands of the classroom.

Break Tasks into Manageable Steps: Many high-functioning autistic children can become overwhelmed when presented with large assignments or projects. Help them break down tasks into smaller, more manageable steps. This reduces anxiety and helps them focus on one task at a time.

Use Visual Aids: Visual schedules, checklists, and task boards can be helpful tools in keeping your child organized and focused on their schoolwork. These visual aids allow them to see exactly what they need to accomplish and help them track their progress.

Build in Breaks: Encourage your child to take short breaks while doing homework, especially if they're feeling overwhelmed. A 5- to 10-minute break can help them reset and return to the task with more focus.

Navigating Social Interactions

Social interactions can be one of the most challenging aspects of school life for children with high-functioning autism. Understanding social cues, making friends, and navigating group activities may require extra support.

Teach Social Skills: Social skills don't always come naturally to children on the spectrum, but they can be taught. Role-playing different social scenarios at home—like how to start a conversation, join a group activity, or ask for help—can give your child the confidence to use these skills at school.

Encourage Peer Support: If possible, identify a peer buddy or mentor in the classroom who can help your child navigate social situations. Having a supportive classmate can make your child feel more comfortable and included in group activities.

Provide Structured Social Opportunities: Children with high-functioning autism often do better in structured social environments. Consider enrolling your child in extracurricular activities or clubs where the social interactions are guided and organized. This can help them build friendships in a more predictable setting.

Extracurricular Activities

Extracurricular activities are a great way for children with high-functioning autism to explore their interests, build social skills, and gain confidence. However, not all activities may be a good fit for your child's needs.

Choose Activities Based on Interests: Select extracurricular activities that align with your child's strengths and interests. If your child loves art, consider an art club. If they're fascinated by technology, a robotics team might be a good fit. When your child is engaged in something they enjoy, they're more likely to thrive.

Be Mindful of Sensory Sensitivities: Some activities, like sports or music, may involve loud noises, bright lights, or other sensory triggers. Make sure the activity accommodates your child's sensory needs or choose quieter, more structured options if necessary.

Start Small: If your child is new to extracurricular activities, start with something small and gradually build up to longer or more complex activities. This allows your child to adjust at their own pace and reduces the likelihood of becoming overwhelmed.

CHAPTER 9: DEVELOPING SOCIAL SKILLS

One of the most significant challenges that children with high-functioning autism face is navigating the complexities of social interactions. While these children may excel in academic settings, they often struggle with understanding social cues, managing their emotions, and forming meaningful relationships with peers. Teaching social skills and emotional regulation is crucial for helping your child thrive, not only in school but in everyday life.

The Importance of Teaching Social Skills and Emotional Regulation

Social skills are often considered intuitive by neurotypical individuals, but for children on the autism spectrum, these skills need to be explicitly taught and practiced. High-functioning autistic children may struggle to understand body language, tone of voice, facial expressions, and the unspoken rules of conversation. Additionally, they may have difficulty regulating their emotions, leading to frustration or withdrawal in social situations.

Learning social skills not only helps your child connect with others but also builds their confidence and self-esteem. When they understand how to navigate conversations, read social cues, and regulate their emotions, they are better equipped to form relationships and engage in group activities.

Emotional regulation is equally important. Children with high-functioning autism may experience heightened emotions during stressful situations, leading to meltdowns or social withdrawal.

Teaching your child how to manage their emotions—particularly in response to social stressors—will help them navigate social interactions with greater ease and resilience.

Practical Exercises and Role-Playing Activities to Help Your Child Interact with Others

Developing social skills doesn't happen overnight. It requires consistent practice in a safe and supportive environment. One of the most effective ways to teach social skills is through role-playing and structured exercises that allow your child to practice different social scenarios.

Here are some practical exercises you can try with your child:

Role-Playing Conversations

Role-playing is an excellent way to help your child understand the flow of conversation and practice social interactions in a low-pressure setting. Start by creating simple scenarios, such as greeting a classmate, asking a teacher for help, or starting a conversation with a peer.

Start Small: Begin with basic social exchanges, like "Hello, how are you?" and gradually increase the complexity. For example, you could role-play situations like introducing yourself to a new friend or making a request.

Practice Turn-Taking: Conversations involve turn-taking, something many autistic children find challenging. Practice taking turns during the role-playing, reminding your child to listen and respond after the other person speaks.

Emotional Regulation Exercises

Teaching emotional regulation is critical to helping your child stay calm in social situations. High-functioning autistic children may feel overwhelmed by emotions such as frustration, anxiety, or anger, especially during social interactions.

Identifying Emotions: Start by helping your child identify their emotions. Use visual aids or emotion charts to teach them how different emotions look and feel. You can ask questions like, "What does your body feel like when you're angry?" or "What do you notice when you're feeling happy?"

Deep Breathing and Calming Techniques: Teach your child simple calming techniques, such as deep breathing or progressive muscle relaxation, to help them manage intense emotions. Practicing these techniques regularly will help them apply them during moments of social stress.

Understanding Personal Space

Children on the autism spectrum often have difficulty understanding personal space and appropriate physical boundaries in social interactions. Role-playing activities can help your child understand the concept of personal space and how to respect the boundaries of others.

The "Hula Hoop" Method: Explain personal space by imagining that everyone has an invisible hula hoop around them, representing their personal space. Practice standing at different distances from each other and asking your child which distance feels comfortable. This helps them visualize the space they should maintain when interacting with others.

Practicing Social Scenarios

As your child gains confidence in basic social interactions, practice more complex scenarios. These might include how to handle disagreements with a friend, how to ask to join a group activity, or how to manage a situation where they don't understand what someone is saying.

Dealing with Misunderstandings: Autistic children may struggle when they misunderstand someone's intentions or words. Practice how to respond calmly when they don't understand something, such as asking for clarification or saying, "I didn't understand that. Can you explain?"

Handling Rejection: Social rejection can be particularly difficult for autistic children. Role-play scenarios where they may face rejection—such as a peer declining an invitation to play—and help them practice responding in a calm and healthy manner. Encourage them to focus on positive alternatives, like finding a different friend to play with or choosing a new activity.

Encouraging Friendships and Dealing with Bullying or Social Rejection

While teaching social skills is essential, it's also important to help your child build friendships and navigate the social dynamics of school and other group settings. Many high-functioning autistic children struggle to form and maintain friendships, and they may face bullying or social rejection. Here are some strategies to help your child build meaningful connections and handle social challenges:

Encouraging Friendships

Making friends can be challenging for children with high-functioning autism, but it's possible with the right support and guidance. Here are some ways to encourage positive social connections:

Find Structured Activities: Many autistic children feel more comfortable in structured environments where social interactions are guided by clear rules and expectations. Enroll your child in extracurricular activities, clubs, or sports where they can interact with peers in a more predictable setting.

Teach Conversation Starters: Help your child learn how to initiate conversations with peers. Simple prompts like, "What's your favorite game?" or "Do you want to play together?" can give them the confidence to reach out to others.

Model Positive Social Behavior: Children often learn by observing. Model positive social interactions in your own life by showing kindness, patience, and understanding in your conversations with others. Your child will pick up on these behaviors and incorporate them into their own social interactions.

Dealing with Bullying and Social Rejection

Unfortunately, children with high-functioning autism are sometimes more vulnerable to bullying and social rejection. It's important to address these issues proactively and help your child navigate them in a way that preserves their self-esteem.

Teach Self-Advocacy: Help your child learn how to advocate for themselves when they face bullying or exclusion. Teach them phrases like, "Please stop," or "I don't like that," and practice saying them in role-play scenarios. This empowers your child to stand up for themselves in difficult situations.

Encourage Peer Support: If your child has a trusted friend or peer, encourage that relationship. A supportive peer can provide a buffer against bullying and help your child feel more secure in social settings.

Stay Involved with the School: Bullying can have serious emotional consequences for children on the autism spectrum. Stay in regular communication with your child's teacher or school staff to monitor how they are doing socially. If bullying occurs, work with the school to address the issue quickly and effectively.

Building Confidence Through Social Skills

Teaching social skills and emotional regulation to children with high-functioning autism is an ongoing process that requires patience, creativity, and consistency. By practicing these skills in a safe, supportive environment, your child will gain the confidence they need to navigate social interactions with more ease. Encouraging friendships, guiding them through challenges, and teaching them how to advocate for themselves will not only help them build stronger relationships but also empower them to handle difficult social situations with resilience.

Remember, every child progresses at their own pace. Celebrate the small victories and continue to support your child as they develop the social skills necessary to succeed in school and beyond.

CHAPTER 10: BEHAVIOR MANAGEMENT: HANDLING MELTDOWNS AND DIFFICULT SITUATIONS

Managing challenging behaviors and meltdowns can be one of the most demanding aspects of raising a child with high-functioning autism. These behaviors are not just "tantrums" but often a result of overwhelming sensory experiences, stress, or frustration that your child is unable to express in a more controlled manner. As a parent, it's crucial to understand what triggers these meltdowns and how to respond in ways that help your child regain control.

Identifying Triggers for Meltdowns and Developing Proactive Strategies

One of the most important steps in managing difficult behavior is understanding what causes it. Meltdowns are often triggered by a combination of sensory overload, unexpected changes, or heightened emotional responses. Identifying the specific triggers that set off meltdowns in your child will allow you to implement proactive strategies to reduce their occurrence.

Here are some common triggers for meltdowns in children with high-functioning autism:

Sensory Overload: Loud noises, bright lights, strong smells, or uncomfortable textures can overwhelm a child's sensory system, leading to a meltdown. Identifying the specific sensory sensitivities your child has can help you manage their environment and avoid these triggers.

Changes in Routine: Many children with autism rely on routine and predictability to feel secure. Unexpected changes, such as a sudden change in plans or disruptions in their daily routine, can create anxiety and lead to a meltdown.

Communication Frustration: Difficulty expressing themselves or understanding others can lead to frustration. When a child cannot communicate their needs effectively, they may become overwhelmed and resort to a meltdown as a form of release.

Emotional Stress: Situations that are emotionally overwhelming—such as being teased, feeling left out, or facing failure—can also trigger meltdowns, as your child struggles to cope with their emotions.

Proactive Strategies:

Use Visual Schedules: Create visual schedules that outline your child's day. This helps reduce anxiety around what's coming next and makes transitions between activities easier to manage. If there is an upcoming change in routine, prepare your child in advance using visual cues or social stories. I know I mention visual schedules frequently in this book, but they have been one of the most important tools that have helped us tremendously.

Monitor Sensory Triggers: Pay close attention to sensory triggers in your child's environment. If you know certain sounds, lights, or textures cause discomfort, take steps to minimize or avoid them. This might include using noise-cancelling headphones, dimming lights, or allowing your child to wear comfortable clothing.

Teach Emotional Regulation Techniques: Help your child identify their emotions and develop strategies to manage them. This could include practicing deep breathing exercises, using a "calm down" space, or introducing sensory tools like fidget toys or weighted blankets.

Create a Safe Space: Designate a specific area at home where your child can retreat when they feel overwhelmed. This space should be free from sensory triggers and filled with calming items, like soft blankets, pillows, or soothing music.

How to Respond During a Meltdown: Calming Techniques and De-Escalation

Despite your best efforts to prevent meltdowns, they can and will happen. When your child is in the middle of a meltdown, the way you respond is critical in helping them calm down and regain control. It's important to remember that a meltdown is not a form of manipulation or misbehavior but rather a sign that your child is overwhelmed and needs help to regulate their emotions.

Here are some techniques to use during a meltdown:

Stay Calm: As a parent, your response sets the tone for how quickly your child can recover. It's easy to become frustrated or overwhelmed yourself, but staying calm and composed will help your child feel safe and supported. Speak in a soft, reassuring voice and avoid raising your voice or expressing anger.

Give Them Space: Sometimes, the best thing you can do is give your child the space they need to work through their emotions. If possible, guide them to a quieter area where they can calm down without additional sensory input or distractions. It's important to respect their personal space during this time and avoid physical contact unless they seek comfort.

Use Calming Techniques: Once your child is in a safe space, encourage them to use calming techniques that you've practiced together. This could include deep breathing, squeezing a stress ball, or hugging a weighted blanket. Some children may respond well to being gently reminded to use these tools, while others may need time before they can engage in calming activities.

Offer Reassurance: During a meltdown, your child may feel overwhelmed and scared by their own emotions. Offering verbal reassurance, such as saying "It's okay, I'm here with you," or "We'll figure this out together," can help reduce their anxiety and remind them that they're not alone.

Wait for Recovery: After the meltdown subsides, don't rush to return to the original activity or expectation. Give your child time to recover fully before discussing what happened or moving on to the next task.

Positive Reinforcement Techniques and Behavior Charts

Positive reinforcement is an essential tool in helping children with high-functioning autism learn new behaviors and manage difficult situations. Reinforcing positive behavior not only encourages your child to repeat those behaviors but also builds their confidence and sense of achievement.

Using Positive Reinforcement Effectively:

Praise Specific Behaviors: Rather than offering general praise like "Good job," be specific about what your child did well. For example, say, "I really liked how you took deep breaths when you started to feel upset," or "Great work using your words to ask for help." This helps your child understand which behaviors are being reinforced and encourages them to repeat them in the future.

Offer Tangible Rewards: In addition to verbal praise, offering small, tangible rewards can be a powerful motivator. This might include a sticker, a small toy, or extra screen time. You can create a system where your child earns points or tokens for positive behaviors, which they can then trade for a larger reward at the end of the week.

Create a Behavior Chart: A behavior chart is a visual tool that helps track and reinforce positive behaviors. You can create a chart with specific goals for your child, such as "Stay calm during transitions," "Ask for help when frustrated," or "Complete homework on time." Each time your child successfully demonstrates one of these behaviors, they earn a star or point on the chart. Over time, they can exchange these points for a reward, such as a special outing or toy.

Be Consistent: Consistency is key when using positive

reinforcement. Make sure that you consistently praise and reward the behaviors you want to reinforce, and avoid giving attention to negative behaviors, as this can inadvertently reinforce them.

Example of a Behavior Chart: You can create a simple chart with columns for each day of the week and rows for specific behaviors, like this:

Behavior	Monday	Tuesday	Wednesday	Thursday	Friday	Reward Earned
Used calming techniques	☆	☆				
Asked for help politely	☆	☆	☆			
Completed homework on time	☆		☆	☆		

At the end of the week, review the chart with your child and celebrate their accomplishments. If they've earned enough stars, they can receive a reward of their choice.

Empowering Your Child Through Behavior Management

Handling meltdowns and difficult behavior is a significant part of parenting a child with high-functioning autism, but it's also an opportunity to teach your child valuable skills for managing their emotions and navigating the world around them. By identifying triggers, using proactive strategies, and responding calmly during meltdowns, you can help your child feel more in control and secure.

Positive reinforcement techniques and behavior charts not only encourage good behavior but also give your child a clear sense of progress and achievement. Remember, consistency, patience, and understanding are key in behavior management. With the right tools and strategies, you can empower your child to regulate their emotions, cope with challenges, and develop the resilience they need to succeed.

CHAPTER 11: FOSTERING INDEPENDENCE: LIFE SKILLS FOR HIGH-FUNCTIONING AUTISM CHILDREN

One of the ultimate goals for parents of high-functioning autistic children is to foster independence. Helping your child develop essential life skills not only builds their confidence but also equips them to navigate the world with greater autonomy. While high-functioning autistic children may face unique challenges, with patience and guidance, they can learn to manage daily tasks, make decisions, and solve problems—skills that will serve them throughout their lives.

Teaching Life Skills: Personal Hygiene, Cooking, and Managing Money

Life skills are essential for daily living and self-sufficiency. For children with high-functioning autism, it's important to break down these tasks into manageable steps and provide clear, consistent instruction.

Personal Hygiene

Good personal hygiene is a fundamental life skill that promotes health, confidence, and social acceptance. However, many children with autism may struggle with sensory sensitivities related to hygiene tasks, such as brushing teeth, showering, or combing hair.

Break It Down: Teach personal hygiene in small, clear steps. For example, when teaching your child how to brush their teeth, break the task into steps such as: wet the toothbrush, apply toothpaste, brush the top teeth, brush the bottom teeth, rinse, etc. Visual aids like a picture chart in the bathroom can serve as helpful reminders.

Create a Routine: Consistency is key. Establish a daily routine for hygiene tasks, such as brushing teeth in the morning and before bed, and showering at the same time each day. The more regular the routine, the easier it becomes for your child to adopt the habit.

Accommodate Sensory Sensitivities: If your child struggles with sensory issues, try to accommodate them by adjusting the products or environment. For example, use a toothpaste with a milder flavor or a softer brush if traditional options are too intense. Allow your child to use headphones during a shower if the sound of water is overwhelming.

Cooking

Cooking is an important life skill that fosters independence, and many high-functioning autistic children enjoy the structure and focus that cooking can provide. Teaching your child to prepare their own meals, even simple ones, can empower them to take care of themselves and understand nutrition.

Start with Simple Recipes: Begin with easy, step-by-step recipes that are clear and predictable. Tasks like making a sandwich, boiling pasta, or preparing scrambled eggs are great starting points. Over time, you can gradually introduce more complex cooking tasks.

Use Visual Recipes: Create visual recipes with pictures or icons for each step. This helps your child understand the process and stay on track. For instance, a visual recipe for making a sandwich could include steps like: get the bread, spread the butter, add the cheese, and so on.

Teach Kitchen Safety: Ensure that your child understands kitchen safety, such as using the stove, handling knives, and being aware of hot surfaces. You can start by supervising closely and gradually allowing more independence as they become comfortable.

Managing Money

Teaching your child how to manage money is an essential skill for future independence. High-functioning autistic children can learn the basics of budgeting, saving, and spending with the right guidance.

Start with Real-Life Scenarios: Use everyday experiences, such as grocery shopping or buying something online, to introduce money management. Explain concepts like the value of different coins and bills, how to count money, and the importance of staying within a budget.

Introduce an Allowance: Give your child a small weekly or monthly allowance and encourage them to save for things they want. This teaches the concept of budgeting and delayed gratification. You can also introduce the idea of saving a portion of their allowance for larger purchases.

Use Visual Tools: Create a simple budget chart or use money management apps that are designed for children. This will help your child keep track of what they earn, spend, and save. These tools can also make abstract financial concepts more concrete and easier to grasp.

Encouraging Decision-Making and Problem-Solving

Fostering independence also involves teaching your child to make decisions and solve problems on their own. Children with high-functioning autism may struggle with decision-making due to their need for routine and predictability. However, with support, they can develop the confidence to make choices and handle challenges in their daily lives.

Offer Choices

One way to encourage decision-making is by offering choices

throughout the day. These can be small, everyday decisions, such as choosing what to wear, picking a meal, or deciding which activity to do. The key is to present a limited number of choices, so your child doesn't feel overwhelmed.

For example, instead of asking, "What do you want for lunch?" you can offer two options: "Would you like a sandwich or pasta?" This allows your child to make a decision within a structured environment, helping them build confidence.

Teach Problem-Solving

Problem-solving is a skill that needs to be explicitly taught. Start by presenting small, manageable problems and guiding your child through the process of finding a solution.

Use Visual Problem-Solving Steps: Create a simple visual chart with steps like: identify the problem, think of possible solutions, choose the best solution, and try it out. For example, if your child is frustrated because they can't find a toy, guide them through the steps: "The problem is you can't find your toy. What are some ways you can find it? Could you check your room or ask someone for help?"

Encourage Trial and Error: Teach your child that it's okay to make mistakes and try again. Problem-solving often involves trial and error, and it's important for your child to understand that making mistakes is part of learning. Praise their efforts and persistence, even if the solution doesn't work out perfectly the first time.

Allow for Natural Consequences

Sometimes the best way for children to learn is by experiencing the natural consequences of their decisions. If your child decides not to bring a jacket to school and gets cold, this experience will teach them to make different choices next time. Allowing your child to experience these consequences in a safe and supportive way helps them take ownership of their decisions.

Helping Your Child Take Steps Toward Greater Independence

Building independence is a gradual process, and every small step counts. Encouraging your child to take responsibility for their daily tasks and decisions will prepare them for the future, even if the progress seems slow at first. The goal is to build their confidence and skills so that they can live as independently as possible.

Here are some strategies to foster greater independence:

Set Realistic Goals: Break down larger life skills into smaller, achievable goals. For example, if your goal is for your child to make their own lunch, start by teaching them how to prepare one part of the meal, such as making a sandwich. Once they've mastered that, move on to teaching them how to pack their lunchbox.

Use Positive Reinforcement: Celebrate every step toward independence, no matter how small. Whether it's brushing their teeth without prompting or successfully cooking a meal, offer praise and rewards to reinforce the behavior.

Be Patient and Consistent: Teaching life skills takes time, especially for children with high-functioning autism. Be patient and consistent in your approach. Repetition is key, and your child may need to practice certain skills many times before mastering them.

Gradually Increase Responsibility: As your child becomes more confident in their abilities, gradually increase the level of responsibility. This might mean giving them more control over their daily routine, allowing them to take on new tasks, or encouraging them to make more complex decisions.

A Journey Toward Independence

Fostering independence in children with high-functioning autism is a journey that requires time, patience, and encouragement. By teaching life skills like personal hygiene, cooking, and managing money, and by supporting decision-making and problem-solving, you are helping your child build the confidence and competence they need to thrive. Independence looks different for every child, but with the right support and guidance, your child can take meaningful steps toward greater autonomy and a more fulfilling life.

CHAPTER 12: FAMILY DYNAMICS: MAINTAINING BALANCE AND HARMONY

Raising a child with high-functioning autism brings unique challenges that can significantly impact family dynamics. The emotional, physical, and mental demands on parents and siblings are often heightened, creating stress and tension within the household. However, with the right strategies and support, it's possible to maintain balance, nurture strong family relationships, and find moments of joy in daily life.

How Raising a Child with High-Functioning Autism Impacts Family Relationships

When one child in the family requires additional care, attention, and support, it's natural for family dynamics to shift. Parents may find themselves devoting a large amount of time to managing their autistic child's needs—whether it's attending therapy sessions, coordinating school plans, or handling meltdowns. This can lead to feelings of exhaustion or even guilt, especially if other family members feel neglected or overwhelmed by the focus on one child.

Here are some ways high-functioning autism can impact family relationships:

Emotional Strain on Parents: Parenting a child with high-functioning autism often comes with an emotional toll. The stress of advocating for your child in school, managing difficult behaviors, and meeting their unique needs can create feelings of isolation or frustration. As a result, the relationship between parents may become strained, as the focus shifts almost entirely to the child's needs.

Siblings May Feel Overlooked: Siblings of children with autism may experience feelings of neglect, as much of the family's attention is directed toward the child who requires more support. They might also feel confused or resentful if they don't fully understand their sibling's needs or why they require extra care. These feelings, if left unaddressed, can create tension within the family and affect sibling relationships.

Family Activities Can Become Stressful: Everyday family activities, such as going on outings, having meals, or attending events, can become challenging when one child has sensory sensitivities or social difficulties. This can lead to stress for parents and siblings, as family outings may be cut short or plans may need to change unexpectedly to accommodate the autistic child's needs.

Despite these challenges, it's possible to create a healthy, balanced family environment. Communication, patience, and a focus on everyone's needs can help strengthen family bonds and improve harmony.

Supporting Siblings and Ensuring Their Emotional Needs Are Met

It's essential to recognize that siblings of children with high-functioning autism have unique emotional needs that also require attention. While they may understand that their sibling needs extra support, it's important that they feel seen, valued, and supported as well.

Here are some ways to ensure the emotional needs of siblings are met:

Acknowledge Their Feelings: Siblings may have mixed emotions about their autistic brother or sister. They might feel proud, protective, and loving, but they may also feel frustrated, jealous, or confused. It's important to create a space where they can express these feelings without judgment. Let them know that it's okay to feel this way and that their emotions are valid.

Spend One-on-One Time: Make an effort to spend individual time with each sibling. This could be as simple as a fun day out, a quiet movie night, or a weekend activity. These moments show siblings that they are valued and give them the chance to have your undivided attention.

Involve Siblings in the Process: When appropriate, involve siblings in their autistic sibling's care. This could include explaining their needs, helping them with tasks, or simply playing together. Helping them understand autism will foster compassion and empathy while strengthening the sibling bond.

Create a Support Network for Siblings: Encourage siblings to express their feelings to trusted friends, relatives, or even through sibling support groups. Many communities and organizations offer support programs specifically designed for siblings of children with special needs. These programs provide a safe space to share experiences and learn how to navigate family dynamics.

The Importance of Self-Care for Parents and Finding Moments of Joy in Family Life

Parents are the pillars of their family, and taking care of themselves is crucial to maintaining balance and harmony in the household. However, the intense demands of raising a child with high-functioning autism can leave parents feeling physically and emotionally drained. Self-care may feel like a luxury, but it is an essential practice that allows parents to recharge and approach family life with renewed energy and patience.

Here's how you can prioritize self-care as a parent:

Make Time for Yourself: Carve out small moments in your day to take care of yourself, even if it's just for 15 minutes. Whether it's going for a walk, practicing mindfulness, reading a book, or having a cup of tea in peace, these moments help you recharge and reduce stress. It's not selfish—it's necessary.

Seek Help and Support: Don't be afraid to ask for help, whether from family members, friends, or professionals. Having a strong support system in place can relieve some of the pressure and give you time to rest. Consider hiring a babysitter, attending support groups, or working with respite care services to give yourself a break.

Nurture Your Relationship with Your Partner: If you're raising your child with a partner, make sure to prioritize your relationship. Schedule regular date nights, have meaningful conversations, and support each other emotionally. A strong partnership provides a stable foundation for the entire family.

Celebrate Small Wins: Find moments of joy in everyday family life, even during challenging times. Celebrate the small victories —whether it's your child mastering a new skill, a peaceful family dinner, or a fun outing. These moments remind you of the rewards of family life and help you stay positive during tough times.

Finding Balance and Joy

Above all, remember to find joy in the journey. While the challenges may be great, so too are the rewards of raising a loving, resilient family. By focusing on the strengths and individuality of each family member, you can create a harmonious household where everyone feels supported, valued, and connected.

CHAPTER 13: BUILDING SELF-ESTEEM AND CONFIDENCE

One of the most crucial aspects of raising a child with high-functioning autism is helping them develop a strong sense of self-esteem and confidence. Children on the autism spectrum often face challenges that can impact their self-perception, especially in social situations or academic settings where they may feel "different" from their peers. It's essential to help your child embrace their uniqueness, build resilience, and develop self-advocacy skills as they grow.

Helping Your Child Embrace Their Strengths and Understand Their Uniqueness

High-functioning autistic children often have remarkable strengths—whether it's an extraordinary ability in a specific subject, an incredible memory, or unique creativity. However, they may also struggle with certain challenges, such as social communication or emotional regulation. It's important to help your child focus on their strengths while also recognizing that their differences make them who they are.

Here are some ways to help your child embrace their uniqueness:

Celebrate Their Talents and Interests: Every child has talents, and children with high-functioning autism are no exception. Encourage your child to pursue the things they love, whether it's drawing, math, music, science, or any other hobby. By focusing on their passions and abilities, you help them build confidence in their own identity.

Explain Autism Positively: As your child grows, they will become more aware of how they differ from their peers. When explaining autism, frame it in a positive light. Let them know that everyone has strengths and challenges, and that autism is simply one part of what makes them unique. Highlight their special talents and abilities, showing them how their way of seeing the world is something to be proud of.

Use Role Models: Introduce your child to role models with autism, whether through books, movies, or real-life examples. Show them that many successful, creative, and talented people also have autism. This can help them understand that their differences do not limit their potential for success.

Promoting Positive Self-Esteem and Resilience

Positive self-esteem is the foundation for resilience, allowing your child to cope with challenges and setbacks while maintaining a sense of self-worth. Building self-esteem involves consistent support, encouragement, and teaching your child to recognize their own value.

Praise Effort, Not Just Achievement: Children with high-functioning autism may struggle with perfectionism or feel disheartened when they don't succeed immediately (I've noticed this with my own kids.). Encourage them by praising their effort rather than just the outcome. Let them know that trying their best is something to be proud of, even if the result isn't perfect. This helps them build resilience and the understanding that failure is part of learning.

Encourage Independence: Allow your child to make decisions and take on responsibilities, even if it's in small, manageable steps. Independence helps foster a sense of capability and self-confidence. Start with tasks they can handle, such as choosing their clothes or helping with household chores, and gradually build from there. Celebrate their accomplishments, no matter how small.

Teach Problem-Solving Skills: Children with strong problem-solving skills are better equipped to handle life's challenges. Encourage your child to solve problems on their own, guiding them through the process if needed. By giving them the tools to overcome obstacles, you're helping them build confidence in their abilities to navigate difficulties independently.

Encourage Positive Self-Talk: Teach your child how to replace negative thoughts with positive ones. If they say things like, "I can't do this," or "I'm not good enough," help them reframe those thoughts by encouraging them to say, "I'll try my best," or "I'm learning, and that's okay." Positive self-talk can help your child develop a more resilient mindset and bounce back from challenges.

Teaching Your Child Self-Advocacy Skills as They Grow

As your child grows older, one of the most important skills they will need is self-advocacy—the ability to understand their own needs, communicate those needs, and ask for support when necessary. Teaching your child self-advocacy skills empowers them to navigate school, work, and social environments with greater independence and confidence.

Encourage Self-Awareness: Help your child understand their strengths and challenges. Ask them how they feel in certain situations—whether at school, with friends, or during tasks—and encourage them to identify what makes them feel comfortable or uncomfortable. This self-awareness is the first step toward advocating for themselves.

Teach Communication Skills: Work with your child on expressing their needs in clear and assertive ways. Role-playing different scenarios can help your child practice asking for help or accommodations in a respectful and confident manner. For example, practice asking a teacher for extra time on an assignment or telling a friend when they need some space.

Involve Them in Decision-Making: As your child gets older, involve them in decisions about their education, activities, or social life. Encourage them to share their thoughts about what works best for them and what they might need to succeed. This gives them a sense of control over their own life and builds confidence in their decision-making abilities.

Practice with Real-Life Situations: Help your child practice self-advocacy in real-life situations, such as at school, during doctor's visits, or in social settings. Over time, they will become more comfortable expressing their needs and advocating for accommodations. Remind them that asking for help is not a weakness—it's a strength.

CHAPTER 14: MANAGING TRANSITIONS: FROM CHILDHOOD TO ADOLESCENCE

The transition from childhood to adolescence is a pivotal time for all children, but it presents unique challenges for children with high-functioning autism. This period brings significant changes—physically, emotionally, and socially—which can be especially overwhelming for autistic children who thrive on routine and predictability. As parents, you can help ease these transitions by preparing for the changes that come with puberty, supporting school transitions, and guiding your child through the complex social landscape of their teenage years.

Preparing for the Challenges of Puberty and Adolescence

Puberty is often a confusing and unsettling time for any child, and children with high-functioning autism may find it particularly overwhelming. The physical and emotional changes that come with puberty can feel sudden and difficult to process, especially for children who experience heightened sensory sensitivities. Preparing your child for these changes, providing clear explanations, and creating a supportive environment can help reduce anxiety during this stage of development.

Talking About Puberty:

It's important to start conversations about puberty before your child begins experiencing the changes themselves. Autistic children often appreciate concrete information, so be direct, clear, and honest about what to expect. Many of us remember going through these changes between ages 14 to 16, but today, it seems to happen much earlier. I won't get into why, but let's just say that kids today develop faster during this time. Please don't wait too long, or your child may end up getting the talk and support from other places, like friends or the web.

Use Simple, Straightforward Language: Explain the physical changes that occur during puberty, such as growing taller, changes in voice, body hair development, and menstruation. Avoid metaphors or vague descriptions that might be confusing. For example, rather than saying, "You'll become an adult," describe specific changes like, "Your voice may get deeper," or, "You'll start to grow body hair."

Visual Aids and Social Stories: Many children with high-functioning autism respond well to visual aids and structured narratives. You can create or find social stories that explain puberty in steps, such as growing taller, body odor, and managing hygiene. These tools can help your child understand the changes without feeling overwhelmed.

Managing Sensory Issues with Hygiene:
The physical changes during puberty—such as sweating, oily skin, and body odor—can be uncomfortable for children with sensory sensitivities. It's important to help them manage these changes in a way that feels comfortable and consistent with their sensory preferences.

Introduce Personal Hygiene Gradually: Develop a routine for personal hygiene that includes showering, using deodorant, and brushing teeth. Break these tasks down into manageable steps, and introduce them one at a time if necessary. For example, start with getting your child used to applying deodorant before adding more steps, like washing their face or showering more frequently.

Accommodate Sensory Preferences: Some children may find traditional hygiene products too strong or irritating. Experiment with fragrance-free or hypoallergenic products, and consider allowing your child to choose their own hygiene items. This gives them some control over the process, which can reduce resistance and make it easier to maintain a routine.

Emotional Changes:
In addition to the physical changes, puberty often brings emotional shifts. Children with high-functioning autism may struggle with mood swings or have difficulty identifying and managing their emotions.

Teach Emotional Awareness: Help your child identify their emotions by encouraging them to check in with how they're feeling. Use simple tools like emotion charts or apps that allow them to track their moods. This can help them recognize patterns in their emotions and develop coping strategies for when they feel overwhelmed.

Provide Reassurance: Emphasize that the emotional changes they're experiencing are a normal part of growing up. Many autistic children may worry that their emotions are out of control or unusual. Reassure them that feeling different emotions throughout the day is natural and that it's okay to ask for help when they need it.

Navigating School Transitions: Elementary to Middle School, Middle to High School

School transitions mark another major change during adolescence, often involving a new environment, new teachers, and different expectations. These transitions can be particularly stressful for children with high-functioning autism, who may struggle with the unpredictability of a new setting. Preparing your child for these changes ahead of time is crucial for reducing anxiety and ensuring a smoother transition.

Breaking Down the New Routine:
One of the main challenges of transitioning to a new school is adjusting to a different routine. The structure of middle school or high school often includes multiple teachers, a rotating schedule, and new subjects that require more responsibility and

independence.

Create a Preview of the New Schedule: Help your child get used to the new routine by introducing them to their schedule ahead of time. If possible, request a copy of the class schedule and create a visual aid that shows when and where each class will take place. Practice this schedule with your child before school starts, so they know what to expect on their first day.

Use Orientation Days: Many schools offer orientation days for new students, which can be incredibly helpful for children with autism. These visits provide an opportunity to explore the new environment, meet teachers, and become familiar with the layout of the building. The more exposure your child has to the new school before the first day, the less intimidating it will feel.

Building Independence with Schoolwork:
As children move into middle and high school, they are often expected to take on more responsibility for managing their schoolwork and keeping track of assignments. This shift can be difficult for children who struggle with executive functioning skills, such as organization, time management, and task completion.

Introduce Organizational Tools: Help your child develop organizational strategies that work for them, such as using a planner, creating to-do lists, or setting reminders on their phone. Encourage them to break down larger assignments into smaller tasks, and practice completing these tasks over several days. These tools will help them stay on top of their work and reduce the stress of last-minute deadlines.

Set Up a Homework Routine: Establish a consistent homework routine that your child can follow every day. This might involve setting aside a specific time and place for studying, eliminating distractions, and taking short breaks as needed. A clear structure for completing homework can make the process more manageable and help your child feel more in control.

Handling Increased Social Pressures and Fostering Independence During Teenage Years

Adolescence brings an increased awareness of social dynamics, peer pressure, and the desire for independence. For high-functioning autistic teenagers, navigating these social pressures can be challenging, especially as they work to develop relationships and manage their social image.

Dealing with Peer Pressure:
Teenagers, including those with high-functioning autism, often experience peer pressure as they seek to fit in with their peers. However, they may struggle to understand or resist these pressures, which can put them in uncomfortable situations.

Teach Boundary-Setting: Help your child understand that it's okay to say "no" to situations or activities that make them uncomfortable. Role-play different scenarios where they might face peer pressure, such as being asked to try something they don't want to do, and practice responses they can use to assert their boundaries.

Focus on Their Strengths: Encourage your child to build friendships based on shared interests. Whether they're passionate about video games, music, or a specific academic subject, finding peers who share these interests will give them a sense of belonging and reduce the likelihood of feeling pressured to conform to activities they don't enjoy.

Fostering Independence:
Adolescence is also a time when teenagers start seeking more independence, which can be both exciting and daunting for parents. For children with high-functioning autism, developing independence requires careful planning and support, but it's an essential step in preparing them for adulthood.

Set Realistic Expectations: Encourage your child to take on more responsibilities, but do so gradually and with clear expectations. For example, you might start by having them manage their own morning routine or pack their lunch for school. As they become more confident, give them more tasks, such as handling their allowance, managing their homework schedule, or making simple meals.

Promote Problem-Solving Skills: Independence often involves solving problems on their own. Teach your child to break down problems into smaller steps and work through solutions. For example, if they miss a deadline for an assignment, guide them through how to ask for an extension or how to plan better next time.

Encourage Future Planning: As your child grows older, begin discussing their future goals. Whether they want to attend college, enter the workforce, or pursue a vocational path, talk about the skills they'll need to achieve those goals. Encourage them to take small steps toward independence, like participating in volunteer opportunities or part-time jobs, to build their confidence in navigating the world outside of school.

CHAPTER 15: EXPLAINING AUTISM TO YOUR CHILD: LETTING THEM KNOW WHO THEY ARE

One of the most significant moments in the journey of raising a child with high-functioning autism is the moment when they come to understand their diagnosis. How and when to tell a child that they are autistic is a deeply personal decision for each family, influenced by the child's age, maturity, and the family's belief system. For many parents, the thought of explaining autism to their child can be daunting, bringing up fears of how they will react, whether they will be bullied, or how it will affect their self-esteem.

In our case, this moment came when Maayan was around 10 years old. For years, my wife and I had debated when and how to tell him. My wife felt strongly that we should explain it when he was around 7 years old, believing that early understanding would help him make sense of his feelings and behaviors. I, on the other hand, worried about the potential impact—what if he told his friends and was bullied? What if he started to think less of himself? I feared that the knowledge might discourage him from trying his best.

However, in the end, it was Maayan himself who raised the question. One day, after watching a TV show that mentioned autism, he turned to us and asked, "Am I autistic?" That moment caught me off guard, but it also made it clear that he was ready to know. We told him, and I have to admit, my wife's instinct was right. Knowing he was autistic helped him understand himself better. Since then, we've seen a lot of improvement—not just in his behavior but in his confidence. He felt empowered by understanding why he experiences the world the way he does.

This chapter will provide advice on how to approach this important conversation, share personal insights from our experience, and offer ideas for helping your child embrace their autism in a positive, affirming way.

Deciding When to Tell Your Child

There is no "right" time to tell your child they are autistic. Every child is different, and what works for one family may not work for another. The key is to observe your child's development, emotional maturity, and understanding of themselves.

Consider These Factors:

Maturity Level: Is your child emotionally ready to understand what autism is? Some children may be ready to grasp this concept at a younger age, while others might need more time.

Curiosity: If your child begins asking questions about why they might feel or behave differently from their peers, this can be a sign that they are ready to know more about their diagnosis.

Family Dynamics: Each family has its own belief system and values. It's important to make this decision as a family, taking into account your child's needs and what feels right for everyone involved.

For us, waiting until Maayan was around 10 years old made sense because he was beginning to notice differences between himself and his peers. He wasn't quite sure what those differences were, but they were starting to affect how he saw himself. When he asked about autism, we knew it was time to give him a clear answer.

How to Explain Autism to Your Child

Once you've decided to tell your child, the next question is how to do it. The goal is to help your child understand that being autistic is just one part of who they are—something that makes them unique and special, not something to be ashamed of.

Keep It Simple and Positive
Depending on your child's age, you'll want to explain autism in simple, positive terms. Focus on what makes them special and unique rather than what sets them apart from others. You might say something like:

"Autism means your brain works a little differently, and that's what makes you really good at certain things, like remembering details or understanding facts about things you love."

"Everyone's brain works differently, and autism is just one way of experiencing the world."

It's important to use language that frames autism as a difference, not a defect. The goal is to help your child see their diagnosis as part of their identity, not something to be fixed or hidden.

Focus on Strengths and Challenges
Every child has strengths and challenges, whether they are autistic or not. Highlight the things your child is good at, while also acknowledging the areas where they might need extra help. For example:

"You're really good at focusing on things you care about, like building with Legos or remembering facts about animals. Sometimes it might be a little harder to understand people's feelings or to make friends, but that's okay—we're here to help you with that."

Use Visual Aids or Books
Children with high-functioning autism often respond well to visual tools or books that help them understand abstract concepts. One idea is to create a personalized book about your child's journey with autism, called something like "Me and My Autism," which explains what autism means and how it relates

to their life. You could include photos, drawings, or stories about their experiences that help them see autism as part of their unique story.

Answer Questions Honestly

Once you tell your child they are autistic, be prepared for questions. They might ask, "Does this mean I'm different from my friends?" or "Why do I have autism?" It's important to answer these questions honestly, but also in a way that reassures them. For example, you can explain:

"Yes, you might experience some things differently than your friends, but that's what makes you special. Everyone is different in their own way."

"Autism is just part of who you are, like having brown eyes or being really good at building things."

Helping Your Child Embrace Their Autism

Telling your child they are autistic is just the beginning of the journey. The next step is helping them embrace their autism and understand that it's something to be proud of, not something to hide.

The Power of Knowing

For us, the decision to tell Maayan about his autism came later than my wife would have liked, but in the end, it was a turning point. After learning he was autistic, Maayan became more comfortable with himself. He understood why he experienced the world differently, and instead of feeling confused or frustrated, he felt empowered. I can't emphasize enough how important it was for him to know who he is.

Every family will approach this conversation differently, and that's okay. The most important thing is that when the time comes, you explain autism in a way that helps your child embrace their unique self, empowering them to grow with confidence and pride.

CHAPTER 16: TECHNOLOGY AND COMMUNICATION TOOLS

In today's world, technology has become an invaluable tool for helping children with high-functioning autism navigate their daily lives. From apps that support communication to visual schedules and assistive devices, technology provides a range of solutions tailored to the unique needs of autistic children. However, as with all things, balance is key—while technology can be highly beneficial, it's important to manage screen time and encourage its productive use.

How Technology Can Help Children with High-Functioning Autism

For many children with autism, technology offers a structured, predictable, and often comforting way to engage with the world. Apps and digital tools are often highly visual and interactive, making them particularly useful for helping autistic children improve communication, social skills, and self-regulation. Here are some key areas where technology can make a difference:

Communication Support:
Children with high-functioning autism may struggle with verbal communication or find it difficult to express their thoughts and feelings in real time. Technology offers a variety of apps designed to support communication, helping children articulate their needs and feelings more easily.

Speech Apps: Apps like Proloquo2Go or AutisMate provide non-verbal or limited-verbal children with tools to communicate using pictures, symbols, and text-to-speech technology. These apps allow children to form sentences by selecting symbols, which the app then translates into speech. Of course, this primarily applies to non-verbal cases, which doesn't typically relate to most high-functioning autistic children. However, there are cases where even high-functioning autistic kids can experience verbal challenges.

Social Stories Apps: Apps like *Stories2Learn* help children understand social situations by providing visual narratives that walk them through different scenarios. These apps are designed to break down social interactions step by step, helping children prepare for situations like making friends, going to the doctor, or dealing with transitions.

Emotional Regulation Tools:
Technology can also help children with autism manage their emotions. There are apps designed specifically to teach emotional regulation strategies, track moods, and provide calming exercises.

Mood Tracking Apps: Apps like *Moodpath* or *Bearable* allow children to track how they're feeling throughout the day. This data can help both the child and their parents identify patterns in their emotions and trigger points, which can lead to more effective emotional regulation strategies.

Calming and Mindfulness Apps: Apps like *Headspace* for Kids or *Calm* offer mindfulness and breathing exercises that can help children calm down during moments of stress or anxiety. These apps provide guided meditations, relaxation exercises, and soothing sounds that children can use to self-soothe when they're feeling overwhelmed.

Learning and Skill Development:
Technology can be a powerful tool for learning, especially for children who respond well to visual and interactive content. Many apps provide structured, self-paced learning environments that are ideal for children with autism.

Learning Apps: Educational apps like *Khan Academy Kids* or

Endless Reader offer engaging, interactive ways for children to build literacy, math, and problem-solving skills. The structured nature of these apps makes learning feel less overwhelming for children who may struggle in traditional classroom settings.

Executive Functioning Tools: Apps like *Remember the Milk* or *Todoist* help children develop organizational and executive functioning skills. These apps allow children to create lists, set reminders, and manage their daily tasks in a way that feels manageable and predictable.

Using Communication Tools: Visual Schedules, Timers, and Assistive Technology

Communication tools play a critical role in helping children with autism navigate their day-to-day activities with greater independence and confidence. Visual schedules, timers, and assistive technology can help reduce anxiety by providing clear, structured expectations.

Visual Schedules:
For many autistic children, visual schedules are an essential tool for managing transitions and understanding their daily routine. These schedules provide a visual representation of what the day will look like, helping children anticipate what's coming next.

Digital Visual Schedules: Apps like *Choiceworks* or *First Then Visual Schedule* allow parents to create customizable visual schedules that children can access on their devices. These schedules can include pictures, icons, or written descriptions of tasks and activities. Many of these apps also offer audio prompts or reminders to help children stay on track.

Benefits of Visual Schedules: Visual schedules give children a sense of control over their day, reducing the anxiety that often comes with changes or surprises. By visually mapping out their day, children know exactly what to expect, which helps them transition between activities with less stress.

Timers and Time Management Tools:

Time management is often a challenge for children with high-functioning autism, who may have difficulty understanding how long tasks take or how to pace themselves throughout the day. Timers and time management tools help children stay on task and manage transitions more smoothly.

Using Timers: Timers, such as *Time Timer* or *Visual Timer*, are excellent tools for helping children understand the concept of time. These timers use visual aids, like color-coded sections, to show how much time is left for an activity. For example, if a child has 10 minutes to complete a task, they can see the time gradually disappear, giving them a clearer sense of how long they have.

Time Management Apps: Apps like *Brili* offer visual time management tools specifically designed for children with autism. These apps break the day into manageable chunks, showing children how long each task or activity will take. The use of visual cues and timers helps children stay focused and manage their time more effectively.

Assistive Technology:
In addition to apps, there are various forms of assistive technology that can help children with autism communicate and participate in everyday activities more effectively.

AAC Devices (Augmentative and Alternative Communication): AAC devices provide alternative ways for children to communicate if they struggle with verbal communication. These devices can range from simple picture boards to more advanced technology that converts text or symbols into speech.

Wearable Technology: Devices like *AngelSense* or *Autism Glass* provide wearable technology that helps children with autism navigate their environment. For example, *AngelSense* offers a GPS tracking device for children who may be prone to wandering, while *Autism Glass* helps children interpret social cues by providing real-time feedback on facial expressions.

Managing Screen Time and Encouraging

Productive Use of Technology

While technology can be an invaluable tool for children with autism, it's important to manage screen time carefully. Like all children, those with autism may be drawn to screens for entertainment, which can lead to overuse if not monitored. However, with mindful management, you can encourage your child to use technology productively.

Set Boundaries on Screen Time:
It's important to establish clear boundaries for screen time, particularly when it comes to non-productive use of technology (such as video games or passive entertainment). Setting limits can help ensure that your child uses technology as a tool for learning, communication, and self-regulation, rather than becoming overly dependent on it for entertainment.

Use Screen Time Tracking Tools: Many devices and apps offer built-in screen time tracking tools, such as *Apple Screen Time* or *Google Family Link*. These tools allow you to monitor how much time your child is spending on different apps and set daily limits for specific types of activities.

Create a Balanced Tech Routine: Structure your child's day to include both screen time and non-screen activities. For example, you can set a rule that for every hour spent on productive screen activities (such as learning apps or communication tools), they should engage in an hour of non-tech activities, such as outdoor play, reading, or family time.

Encourage Productive Use of Tech:
While it's important to limit screen time, it's equally important to guide your child toward productive uses of technology that align with their interests and needs. Encourage your child to use technology as a tool for learning new skills, exploring their passions, and improving communication.

Explore Creative Outlets: Encourage your child to use technology for creative activities, such as drawing apps, coding platforms, or music composition software. These activities allow them to explore their interests while building valuable skills.

Promote Interactive and Educational Content: Rather than passive screen time (like watching YouTube or playing video games), encourage your child to engage with interactive and educational apps that challenge them to think critically, solve problems, or create something new.

CHAPTER 17: OVERCOMING CHALLENGES AND CELEBRATING WINS

Raising a child with high-functioning autism is a journey filled with highs and lows. From the everyday struggles of managing routines and communication to the moments of triumph when your child achieves something they've worked hard for, the emotional rollercoaster can feel overwhelming. Yet, it's often the small victories and moments of progress that bring the greatest joy and keep us moving forward. While every family faces challenges, it's important to find strategies to overcome them and, most importantly, to celebrate every win, no matter how small.

Common Challenges Families Face and How to Overcome Them

Every family raising a child with high-functioning autism will encounter their own set of challenges. Some days may feel like a constant battle, whether it's dealing with difficult behaviors, managing sensory overload, or navigating the school system. While these challenges are inevitable, developing strategies to address them can help ease the pressure and create a more positive environment for both parents and children.

Managing Behavioral Challenges

Behavioral issues are one of the most common challenges parents face, especially when children struggle with emotional regulation or sensory overload. Meltdowns, rigidity in routines, and resistance to change can make day-to-day life difficult.

Strategy: Consistency and Predictability

One of the best ways to manage behavioral challenges is by providing consistency and predictability in your child's routine.

Having a set schedule and clear expectations can reduce anxiety and help your child feel more secure. When possible, prepare your child for any changes in advance to minimize resistance.

Strategy: Break Down Tasks

Large tasks can feel overwhelming, and sometimes what seems like minor resistance is your child struggling with the complexity of the task. Break tasks down into smaller steps and provide positive reinforcement as they complete each step. For example, instead of saying, "Clean your room," break it down into "Pick up the toys, put your clothes in the basket, and make your bed." This helps make the task feel more achievable.

Addressing Social Isolation and Rejection

Social challenges are another area where families often struggle. Children with high-functioning autism may have difficulty forming friendships or understanding social cues, which can lead to feelings of isolation or rejection.

Strategy: Focus on Structured Social Activities

Social interactions in free-form environments (like recess or unstructured playtime) can feel chaotic for children on the spectrum. Structured activities like clubs, sports, or hobby groups provide a more predictable environment where children can practice social skills while focusing on something they enjoy. This helps reduce anxiety and encourages positive social connections.

Strategy: Role-Playing and Social Stories

Practice social situations at home through role-playing or using social stories to explain different scenarios. By walking through these situations in a safe environment, your child will be better prepared to handle them in real life. You can role-play common interactions, such as joining a group at lunch, asking to play with a friend, or handling rejection.

Overcoming Communication Barriers

Even for high-functioning children, communication can sometimes be a struggle. Whether it's difficulty expressing feelings or misunderstanding non-verbal cues, communication barriers can lead to frustration and misunderstanding.

Strategy: Use Visual Communication Tools
If your child finds it difficult to express themselves verbally, visual tools like emotion charts or apps that allow them to point to images or words can help bridge the communication gap. These tools allow your child to express how they're feeling or what they need without relying solely on verbal communication.

Strategy: Encourage Self-Advocacy
Teaching your child self-advocacy skills can empower them to ask for what they need, whether in school, at home, or in social situations. Work with your child on how to communicate their needs clearly and respectfully, whether it's asking for a break during a meltdown or requesting help with a difficult task.

Celebrating Milestones, No Matter How Small

In the whirlwind of daily challenges, it's easy to overlook the progress your child is making. However, every small achievement is worth celebrating. Whether it's a behavioral improvement, a social breakthrough, or mastering a new skill, these moments deserve recognition. Celebrating milestones not only boosts your child's confidence but also reminds you of the progress that's happening—even if it feels slow at times.

Acknowledge Effort, Not Just Success
It's important to recognize your child's effort, even if the outcome isn't perfect. Did your child try a new food for the first time? Did they attempt to participate in a group activity at school? Even if the experience wasn't flawless, acknowledging their effort encourages them to keep trying.

Celebrate Progress Over Perfection: Focus on how far your child has come rather than comparing them to neurotypical children or expecting perfection. Progress might look like your child saying "hi" to a classmate, even if they don't engage in a full conversation. These moments matter, and they build the foundation for future growth.

Create a "Victory Journal"

One idea for celebrating wins is to create a "Victory Journal." This can be a simple notebook where you jot down each new milestone or achievement your child reaches, no matter how small. You could also include photos or drawings of your child's successes. Looking back on this journal during challenging times can remind you of how much progress your child has made over the years.

Make Celebrations Special

When your child achieves a milestone—whether it's learning to tie their shoes, making a new friend, or completing a school project—celebrate it in a way that's meaningful to them. This could be as simple as letting them choose a special activity for the day, going out for a treat, or giving them a small reward. These celebrations reinforce the idea that effort and progress are valued and encourage them to keep pushing forward.

CHAPTER 18: YOU'RE NOT ALONE—A MESSAGE OF HOPE

As we come to the end of this book, I want to take a moment to speak directly to you—the parent reading this, who may be navigating the emotional rollercoaster that comes with raising a high-functioning autistic child. If there's one thing I've learned from my own journey, it's that every family's experience is unique, but the highs and lows we face are universal. Some days are filled with joy and pride, while others can feel overwhelming. But through it all, one message remains clear: **you are not alone**.

A Personal Reflection on Our Journey

My own family's journey has been filled with both triumphs and challenges. As I've shared throughout this book, my wife Adi and I faced many difficult decisions as we raised our son Maayan. From debating when to tell him he was autistic to moving our family to Thailand in search of a better educational environment, our journey has been anything but linear. There have been moments when we questioned ourselves, times when it felt like we weren't making progress, and days when the challenges seemed insurmountable.

But with every low came moments of growth and discovery. Maayan, and his younger brother Gal, have taught us more than we could have ever imagined. They've taught us patience, resilience, and the beauty of seeing the world through a different lens. Having an autistic child has been the greatest teacher of all, and despite the difficulties, I can honestly say that **having an autistic child has been the best thing that ever happened to me**.

I've learned that success doesn't happen overnight. It takes time, sometimes a long time. But those small steps forward—the first time Maayan asked a friend to play, the moment he realized he was capable of so much more than he thought—are the moments that make every struggle worthwhile.

If you're feeling overwhelmed or unsure, know that it's okay. It's normal. And it's part of the process. There will be highs, and there will be lows. But in the long run, these children are incredible teachers, showing us what unconditional love, perseverance, and understanding really mean.

Key Messages from the Book

As you reflect on your own journey, I want to recap some of the key messages from this book:

Celebrate Every Win, No Matter How Small: Progress might be slow, but every achievement, no matter how small, is a victory. Whether it's mastering a new skill, handling a social situation better, or simply having a good day, these moments deserve celebration. They are signs of growth.

You Are Your Child's Biggest Advocate: Your voice matters. Whether it's working with teachers, doctors, or other professionals, you are your child's advocate. Trust your instincts, push for the support your child needs, and never be afraid to stand up for what you know is best for them.

Take Time for Yourself and Your Relationships: Raising a child with high-functioning autism can take up so much of your time and energy that it's easy to lose sight of your own needs or the needs of your relationship. But taking care of yourself is essential. You are a better parent when you take time to recharge, spend time with your partner, and nurture your own mental and emotional well-being.

Your Child's Future is Bright: No matter what path your child takes—whether they pursue vocational training, higher education, or something entirely different—the future is full of possibilities. Focus on your child's strengths, support their passions, and help them build the skills they need to live a fulfilling life, whatever that looks like for them.

It's Okay to Ask for Help: You don't have to do this alone. Whether you seek out support groups, family, friends, or professionals, reaching out for help is a sign of strength, not weakness. Surround yourself with people who understand and support your journey.

Embracing the Ups and Downs

If there's one truth about parenting a high-functioning autistic child, it's that the journey is filled with ups and downs. Some days you'll feel like you're making incredible progress, and other days will feel like you're back at square one. But it's all part of the process.

I've learned that it's okay to embrace those challenging days. They don't define you as a parent, nor do they define your child's potential. The struggles are just moments in time, and they are often the moments that help us grow the most. On the other hand, the highs—the moments of joy, laughter, and pride—are what give us the strength to keep going.

No matter how hard things may seem, remember that your efforts are making a difference. Every time you advocate for your child, every time you teach them a new skill, and every time you help them navigate the world, you are contributing to their success.

You Are Not Alone

If there's one thing I want to leave you with, it's this: **you are not alone**. There are countless families walking this path alongside you. We all share the same fears, hopes, frustrations, and triumphs. And while no two journeys are exactly the same, we are united by our love for our children and our desire to help them thrive.

As you continue on this journey, don't forget to reach out for support when you need it. Share your victories and your struggles with others who understand. Celebrate the milestones, even the smallest ones. And above all, know that you are doing an incredible job.

Raising a child with high-functioning autism is not easy, but it is deeply rewarding. These children have a way of teaching us what really matters in life—patience, understanding, and unconditional love. They show us how to see the world in new and beautiful ways, and for that, they are our greatest teachers.

Printed in Great Britain
by Amazon

8981a4b3-a69c-42e2-a84b-54ba6e7a1f9aR01